Reimagining a Museum for the 21st Century

Arkansas Museum of Fine Arts

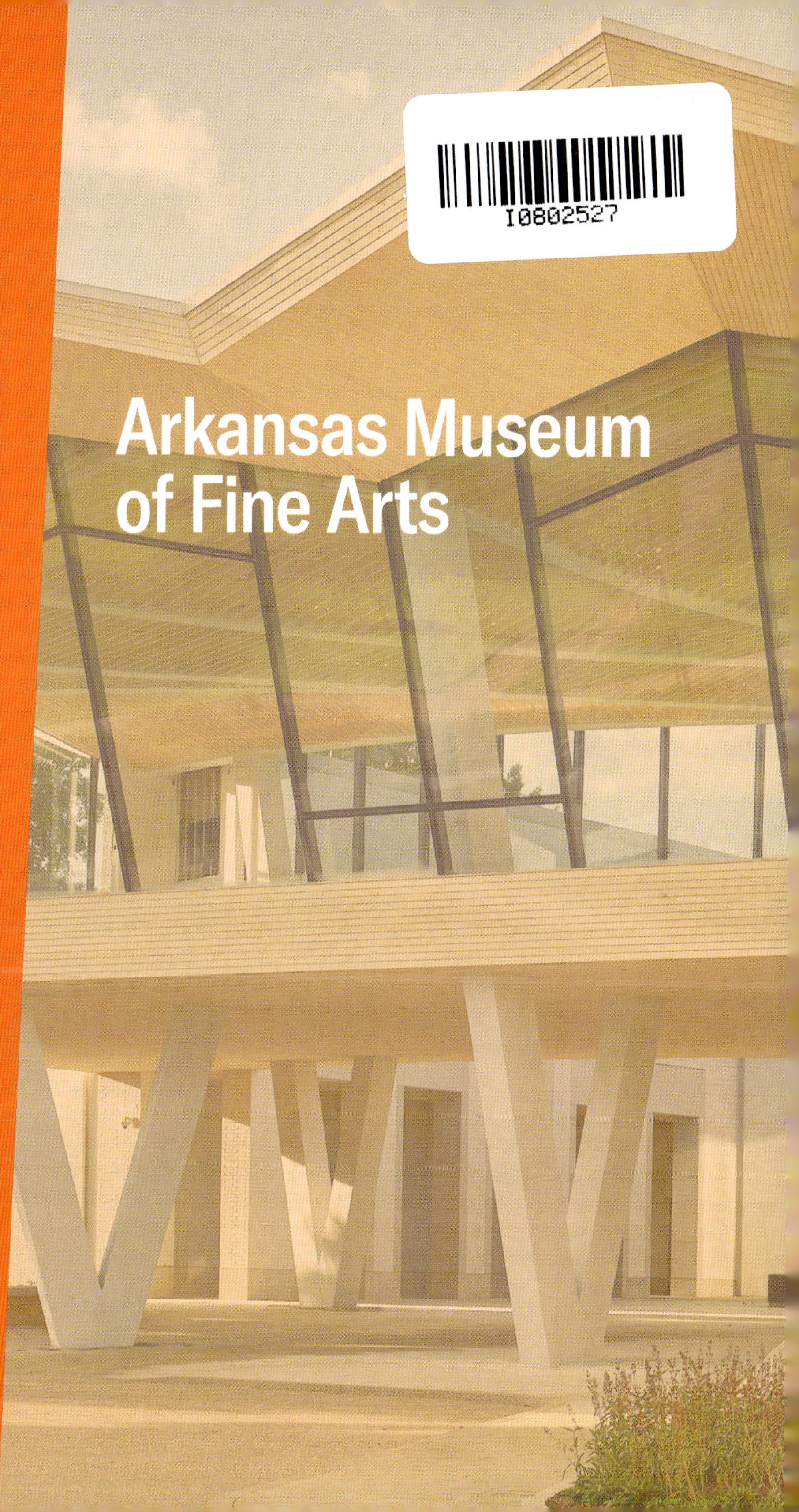

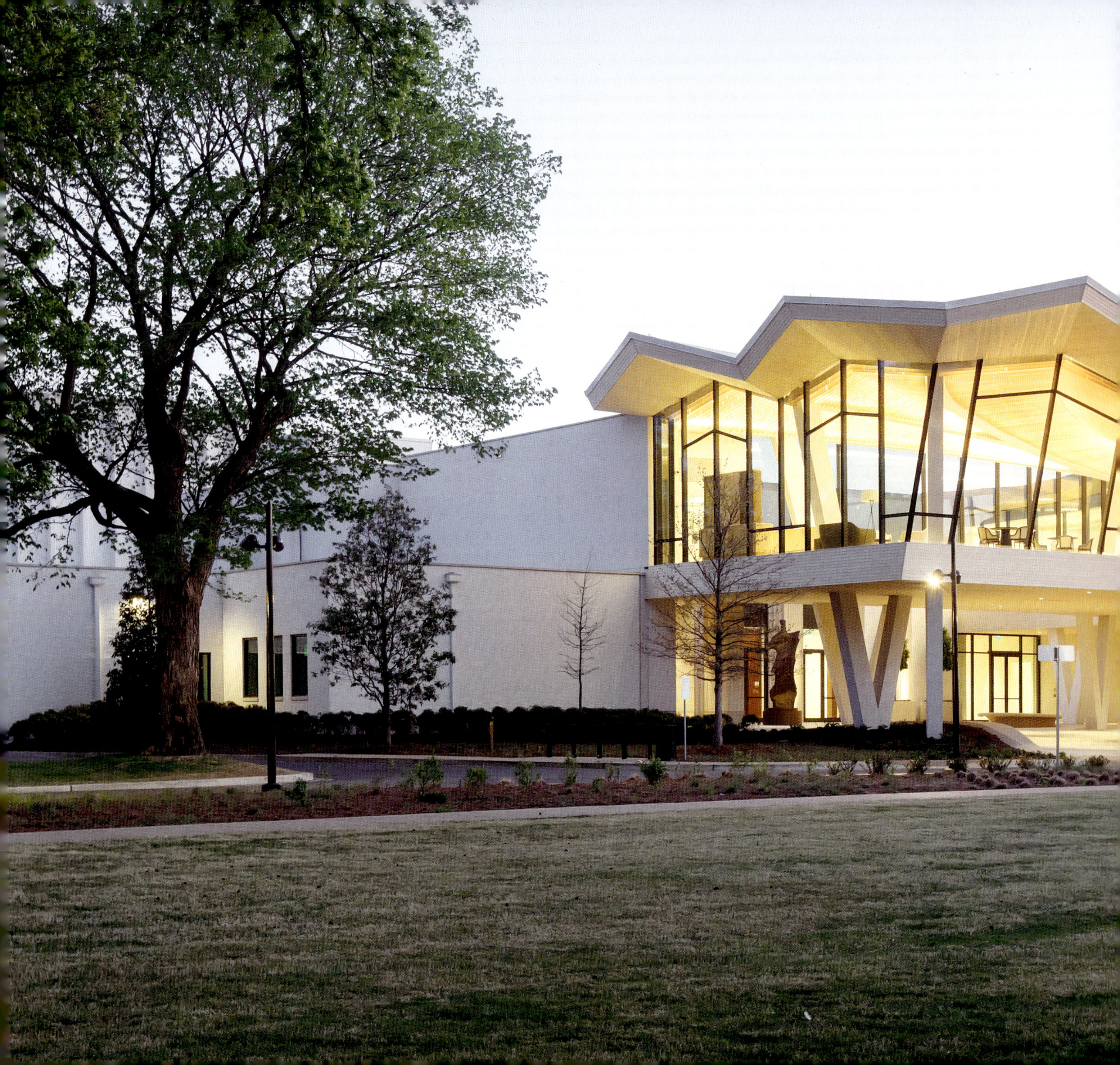

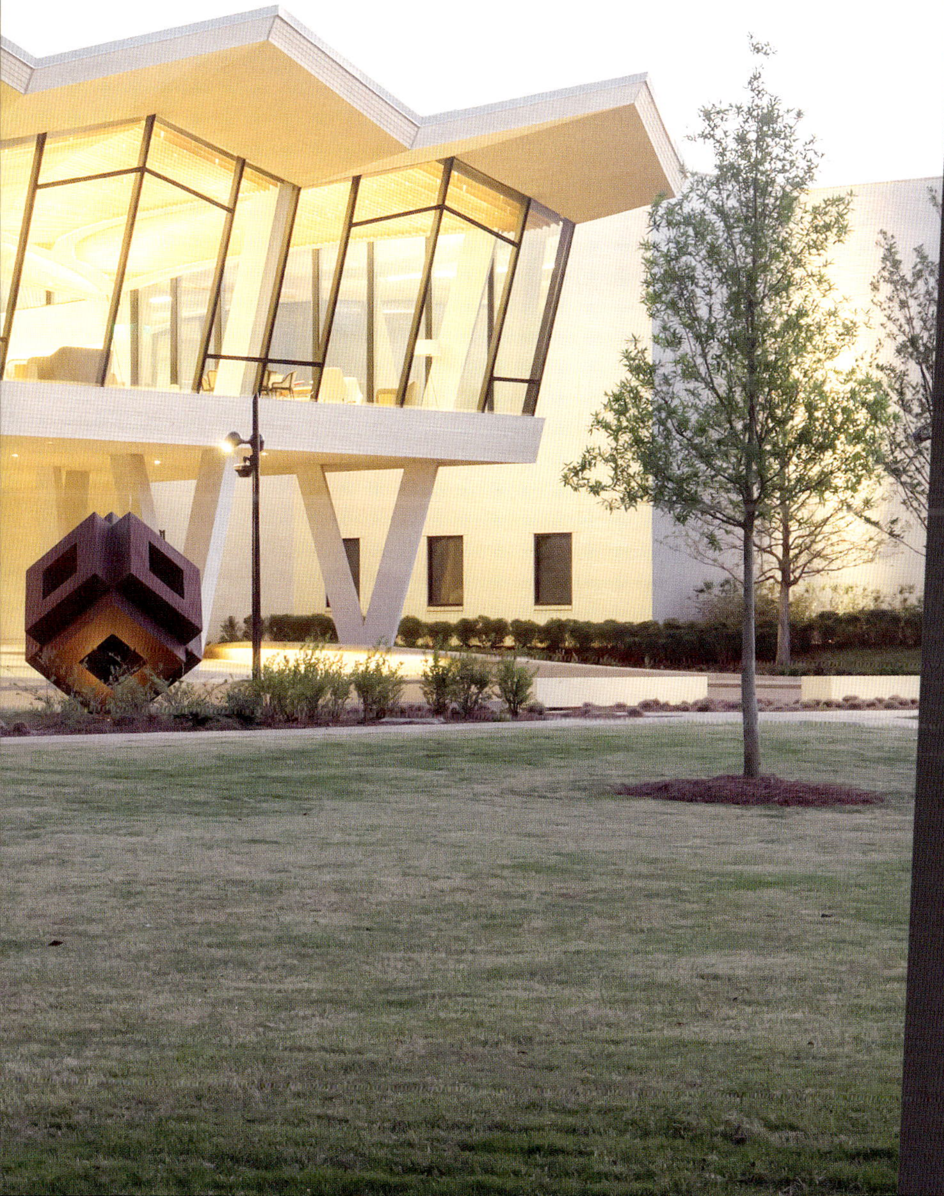

Arkansas Museum of Fine Arts

Reimagining a Museum for the 21st Century

CONTENTS

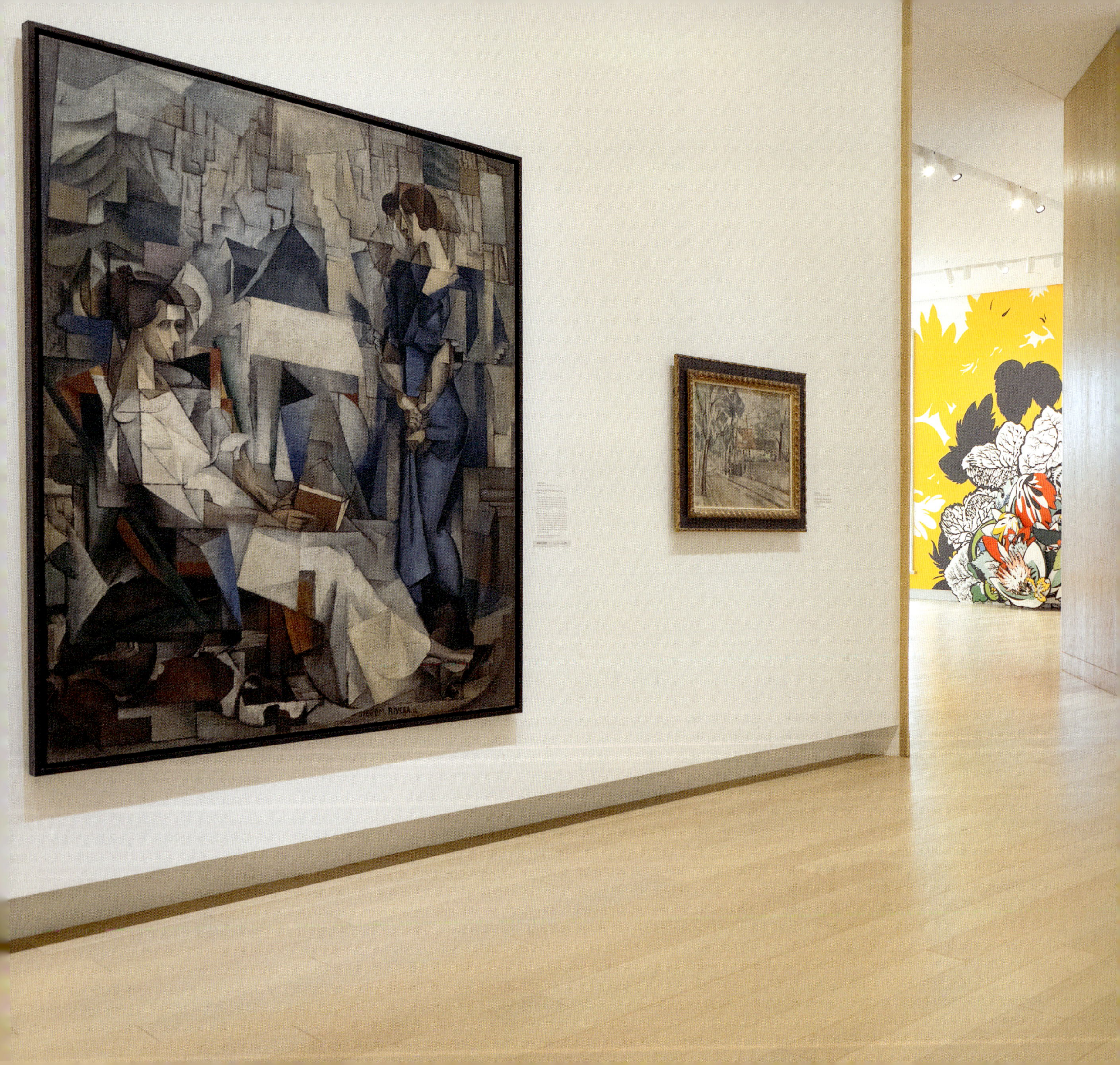

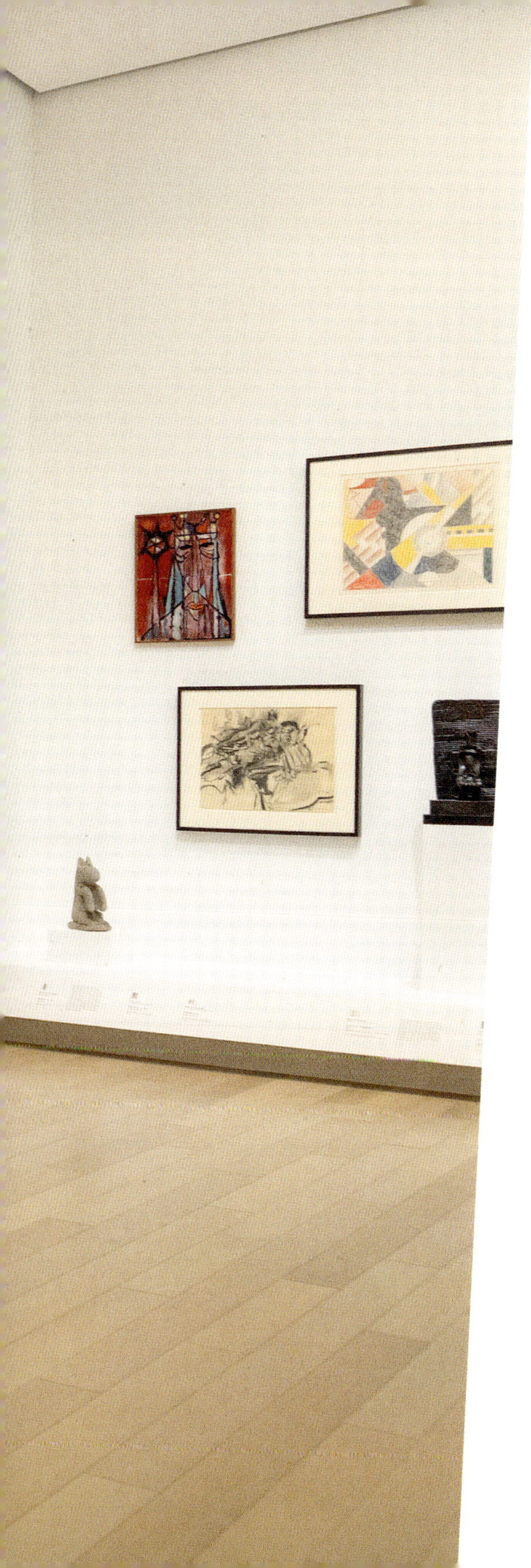

A Destination for Culture and Community

The transformed Arkansas Museum of Fine Arts (AMFA) welcomes all to make, view, and experience visual and performing arts. The dynamic and inviting building, opened in 2023, is designed to encourage social interactions among visitors and features flexible spaces that foster the interdisciplinary programming that has been AMFA's hallmark since the 1960s. Windows throughout the building offer views onto nature, framing the surrounding park setting, landscape of native plants, and outdoor sculpture across 11 acres.

Founded in 1937 and located in Little Rock's oldest urban green space, MacArthur Park, AMFA offers a unique blend of visual and performing arts experiences. The AMFA Foundation's 14,000-object international collection spans seven centuries, with strengths in works on paper and contemporary craft, and includes notable holdings by artists from Arkansas, the wider Mississippi River Delta region, and the United States and Europe. Children's Theatre and Performing Arts, established in 1979,

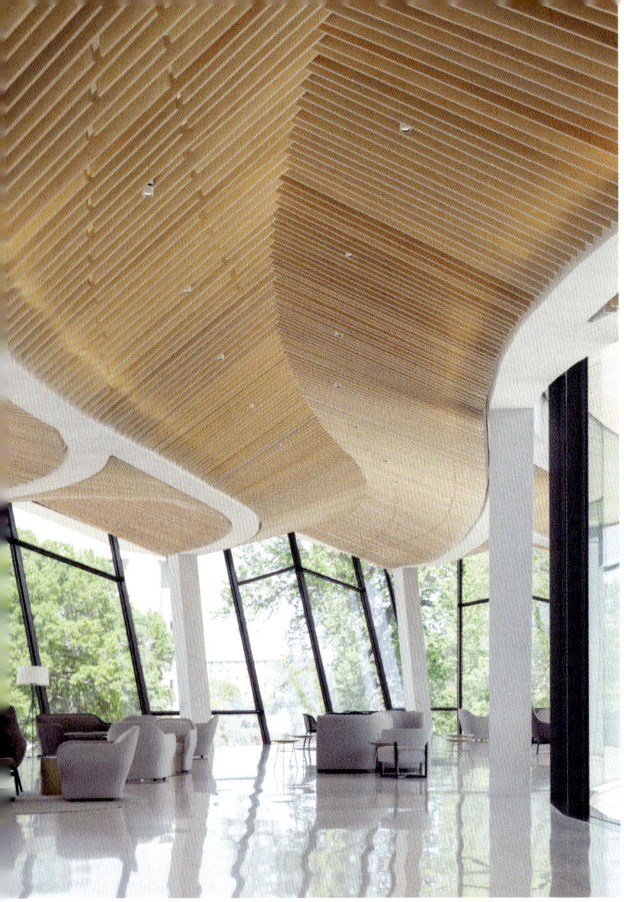

presents a range of productions for all ages. Families enjoy a decades-long tradition of contemporary and classic literary stories adapted by AMFA for the stage as well as productions by national and international touring companies. Established in 1963, AMFA's Windgate Art School offers expanded studio curricula in drawing, painting, ceramics, glass, metals, woodworking, and other media. Instruction is available for students of all ages and skill levels, with daytime and evening classes as well as short-term courses, youth academies, and specialty workshops. An artist-in-residence program welcomes established and emerging artists to teach and create in the Art School studios. General admission to AMFA is always free.

In early 2016, Little Rock residents voted overwhelmingly for a hotel tax to support AMFA's reimagined building. That December, a committee of representatives from the community, the city of Little Rock, and AMFA's Board and Foundation selected Chicago-based Studio Gang as the architect. Led by MacArthur Fellow Jeanne Gang,

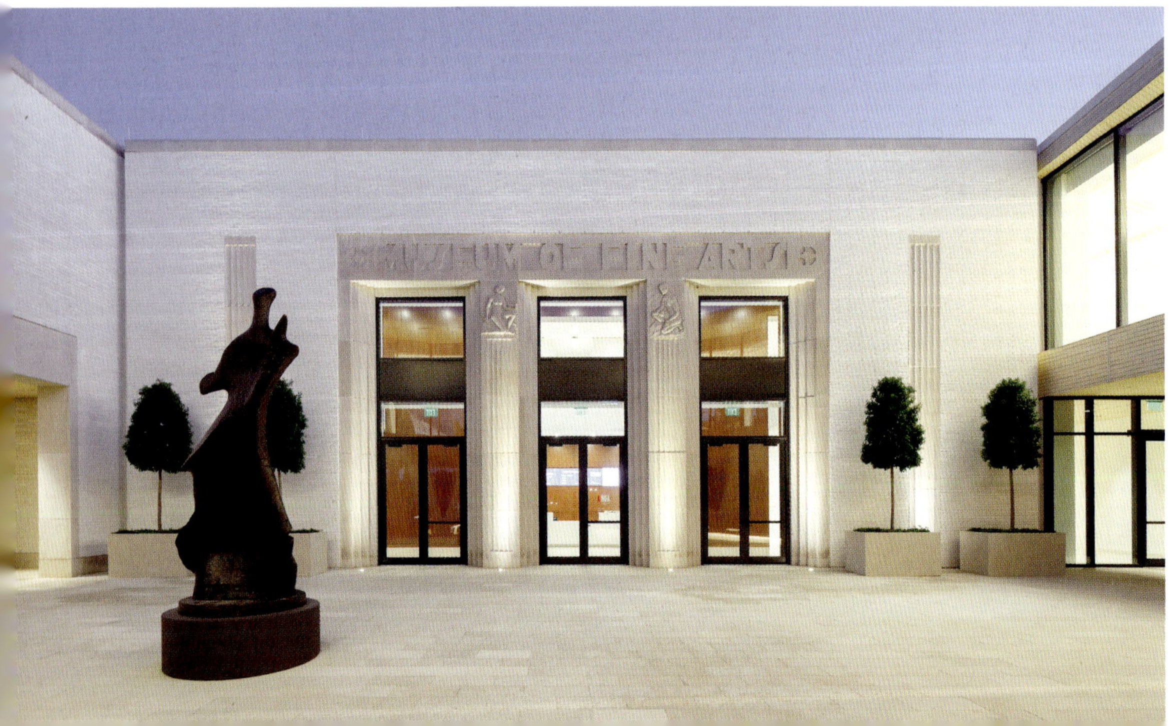

The 1937 façade of the Museum of Fine Arts (pictured in 2023 at left and in an undated historical photo below) features two carved-limestone reliefs, *Painting* and *Sculpture* personified, designed by Little Rock artist Benjamin D. Brantley. The Art Deco entrance welcomes visitors from the adjacent Courtyard.

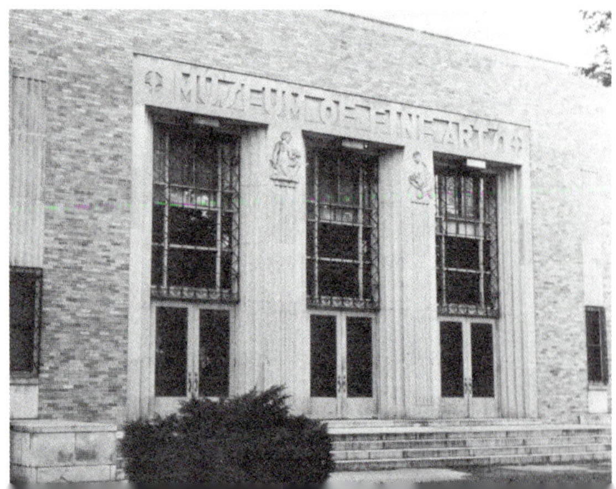

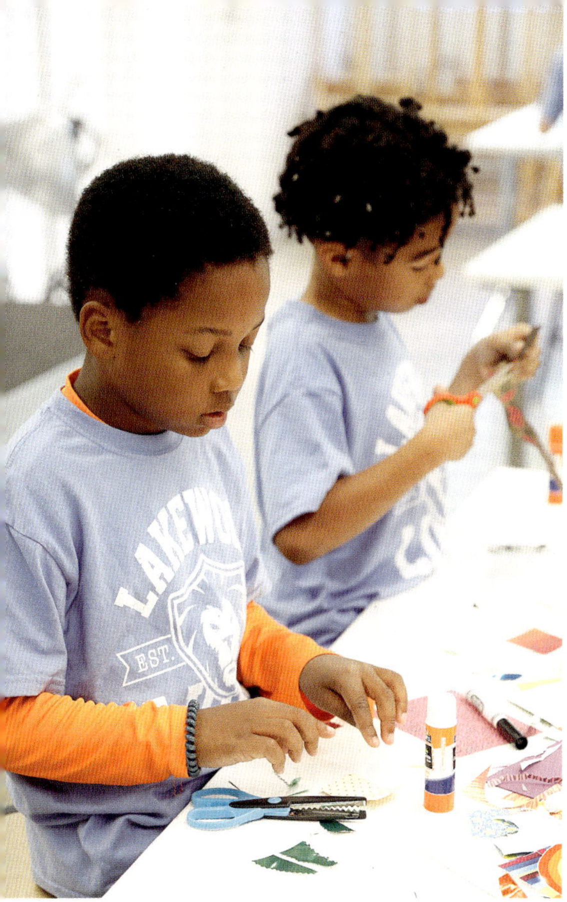

AMFA offers children a variety of playful educational experiences that cultivate curiosity and foster a love of the arts.

the firm stood out for its commitment to sustainability, its elegant and thoughtful approach to architecture, its understanding of the site's challenges and opportunities, and its vision for AMFA as a cultural beacon. New York City firm SCAPE, led by MacArthur Fellow Kate Orff, was chosen as landscape architect.

Studio Gang's design lends a new, highly visible architectural identity to AMFA, while SCAPE's plan for the Museum grounds draws inspiration from Little Rock's unique regional ecologies—including the banks of Fourche Creek, the bluffs of Emerald Park, and the agrarian landscapes of the Mississippi Delta. Built in eight different additions beginning in 1937, the former Museum building enclosed noncontiguous galleries and programming spaces. For the reimagined AMFA, Studio Gang conceived an Atrium that opens to the Courtyard Entrance at the north and runs to the Park Entrance at the south, creating a unifying axis that clarifies circulation and makes visible the Museum's program areas—art galleries, studio classes, and the performing arts. The design also connects the institution's history to its vision for the future. At the north, the 1937 Art Deco façade, which had been enclosed inside the galleries since 1982, is now the Courtyard Entrance. The Cultural Living Room overlooks the historic façade and greets visitors with a dynamic presence. To the south, the light-filled restaurant and Park Entrance open onto SCAPE's revitalized landscape, featuring native and sustainable plantings, pathways, and sculpture.

AMFA reopened its doors to the public in April 2023, welcoming visitors to enjoy their museum experience in a reimagined building. Full of spaces to inspire looking, lounging, thinking, and conversing, the Museum has been transformed into a place for connection: the indoors to the outdoors, the galleries to the Art School and Theater, and visitors to one another.

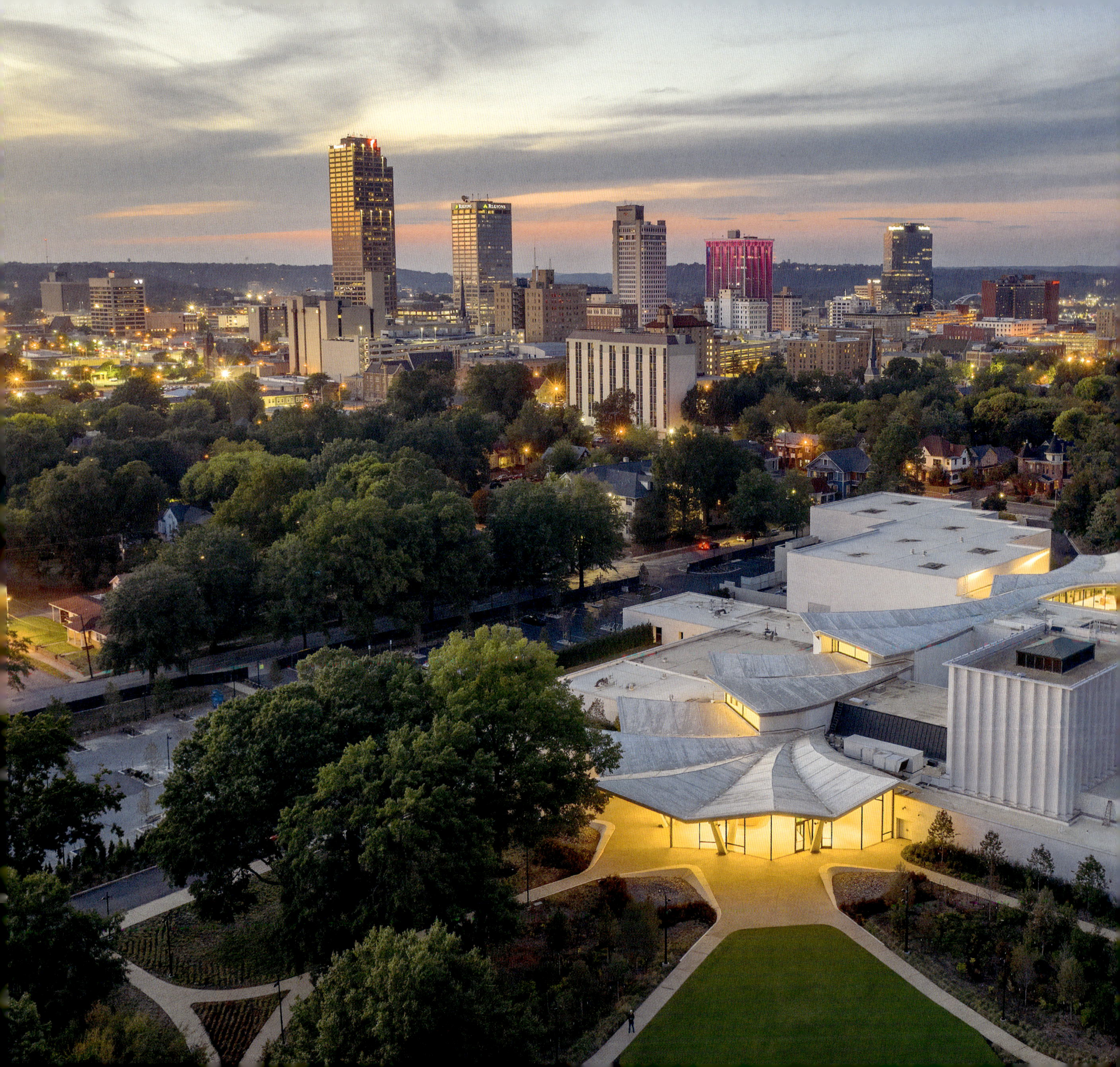

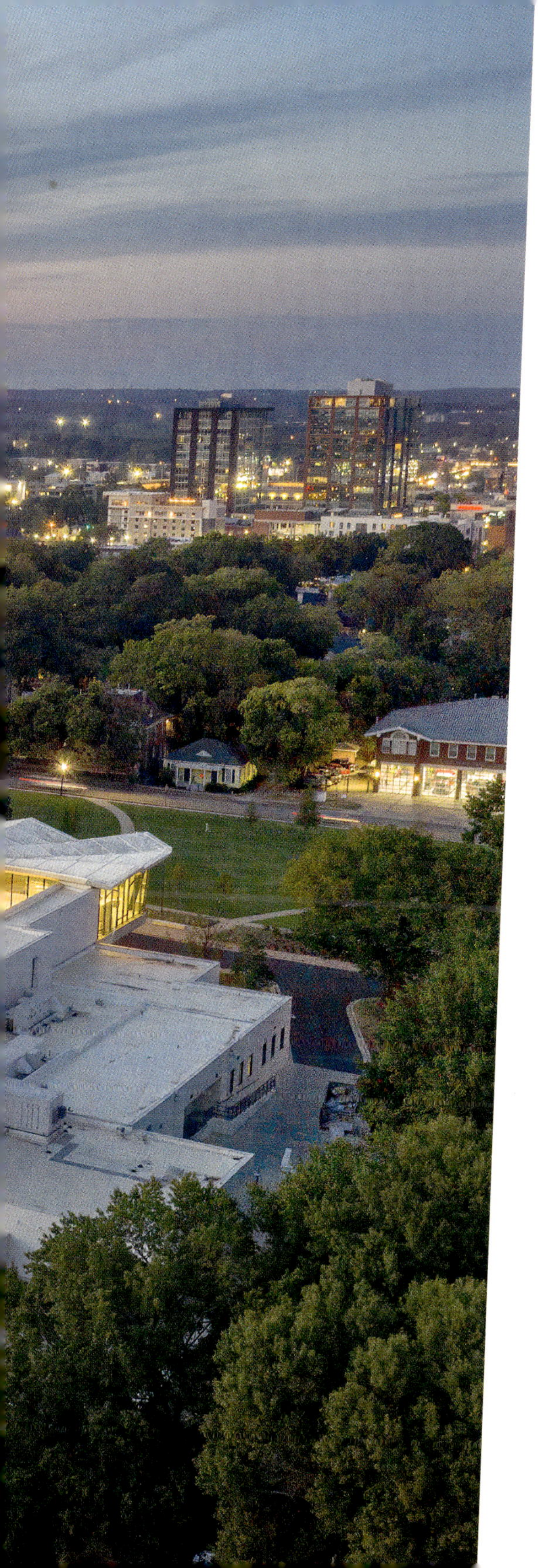

The Museum in Photographs

Bringing together people, art, and nature, the Arkansas Museum of Fine Arts is a vibrant destination for culture and community in Little Rock. Connecting the city, surrounding neighborhoods, and MacArthur Park, the building welcomes everyone to enjoy its diverse collection and programming, and extends the experience of art well beyond its walls.

The former Museum building's eight existing structures, built in different eras and representing several architectural types, now work together as a harmonious whole. At the center of the reimagined AMFA is a new connective space that runs axially through the building, north to south, like a graceful stem. Unifying and reorganizing the Museum's existing functions, it allows a seamless flow through the building and across the site, transforming the visitor experience and greatly improving daily operations. At each end, this central stem appears to blossom outward, presenting an architecture of new, distinct entrances and areas for social functions and programs. Both inside and outside, the organic, curving form offers an elegant response to the constraints of the preexisting structure and foundations, which were preserved as part of the design's sustainable approach.

The fluid lines of the architecture continue into the new pathways and petal-shaped gardens of the Museum's 11-acre grounds, which are part of Little Rock's oldest public park. The design of the gardens, which have been revitalized from the soil up, introduces a range of native plants that distills iconic Arkansas landscapes into shaded spaces that extend out from the building, allowing AMFA to foster renewed ecological diversity along with vital connections between people and art.

Visitors arriving at the Museum from the north encounter the new Cultural Living Room. With its transparent façade and bold, uplifted form, this community gathering space is a welcoming beacon that leads to the adjacent Courtyard.

The folded-plate roof provides both visual interest and structural integrity for the building. Made of cast-in-place concrete, the roof extends beyond the glass walls of the Cultural Living Room, minimizing glare from the sun. Its pleats, clad with wood on the interior, also add warmth and animate the entrance.

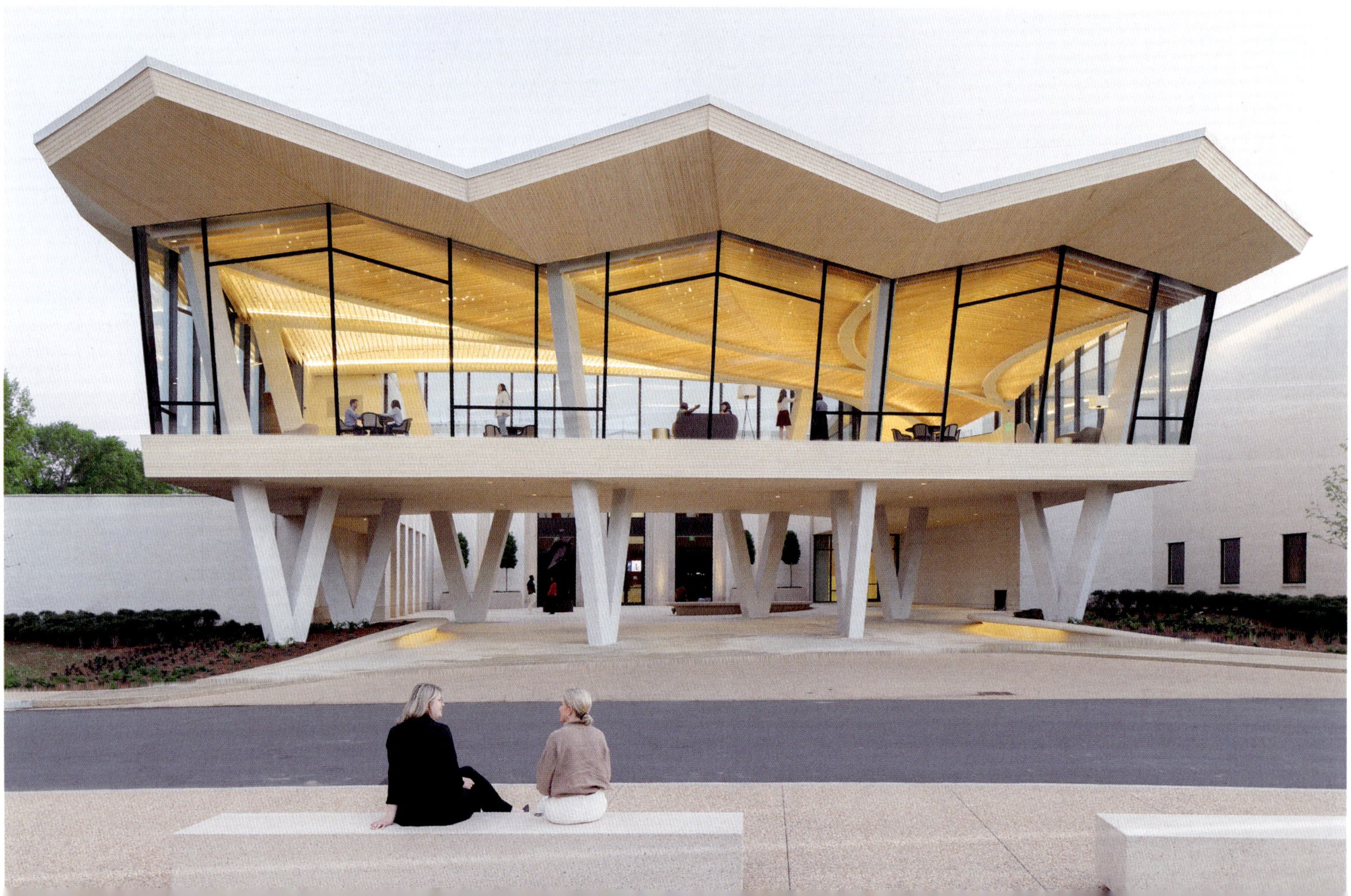

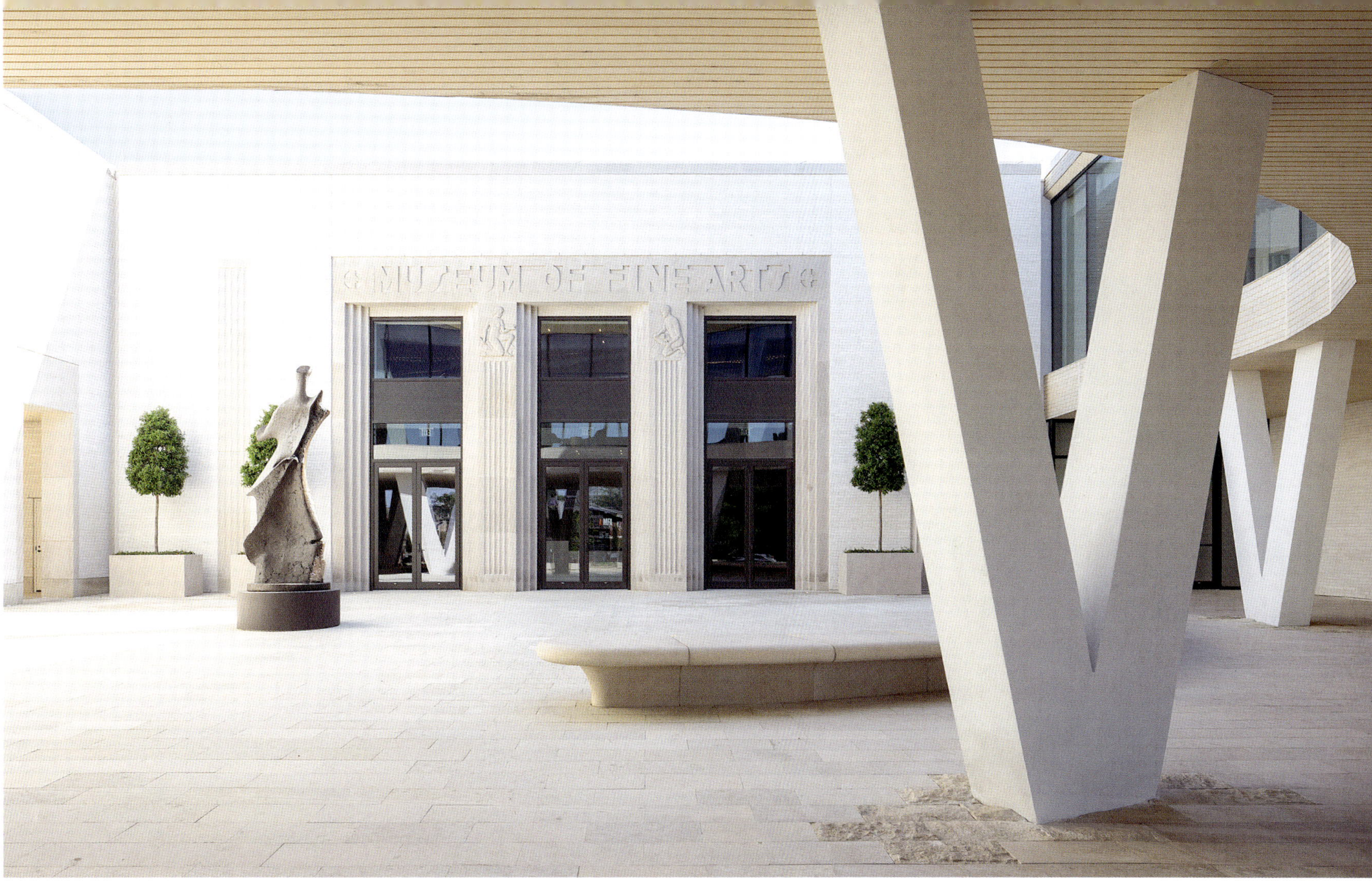

Passing under the Cultural Living Room, visitors enter the Courtyard. Here, the Art Deco façade of the Museum's original 1937 building, enclosed by a previous addition, resumes its function as a grand entryway. The limestone façade features two carved reliefs—*Painting* and *Sculpture* personified—that identify the Museum as a place of art and creativity.

The new Courtyard offers a serene outdoor space for reflection and meeting. A curving, sculptural bench of precast concrete follows the sweeping arc of the Cultural Living Room above. Henry Moore's bronze sculpture *Large Standing Figure: Knife Edge* (1961, cast in 1976) provides a focal point. An abstracted human form inspired by the shape of an avian shoulder bone, the sculpture is on loan from the city of Little Rock and was conserved before its installation in the Courtyard.

The new arcade at the east side of the Courtyard is designed to complement the Art Deco character of the 1937 façade. Sharing the same brick and limestone material and with openings of similar proportions, the arcade provides another shaded respite defining the Courtyard's boundary.

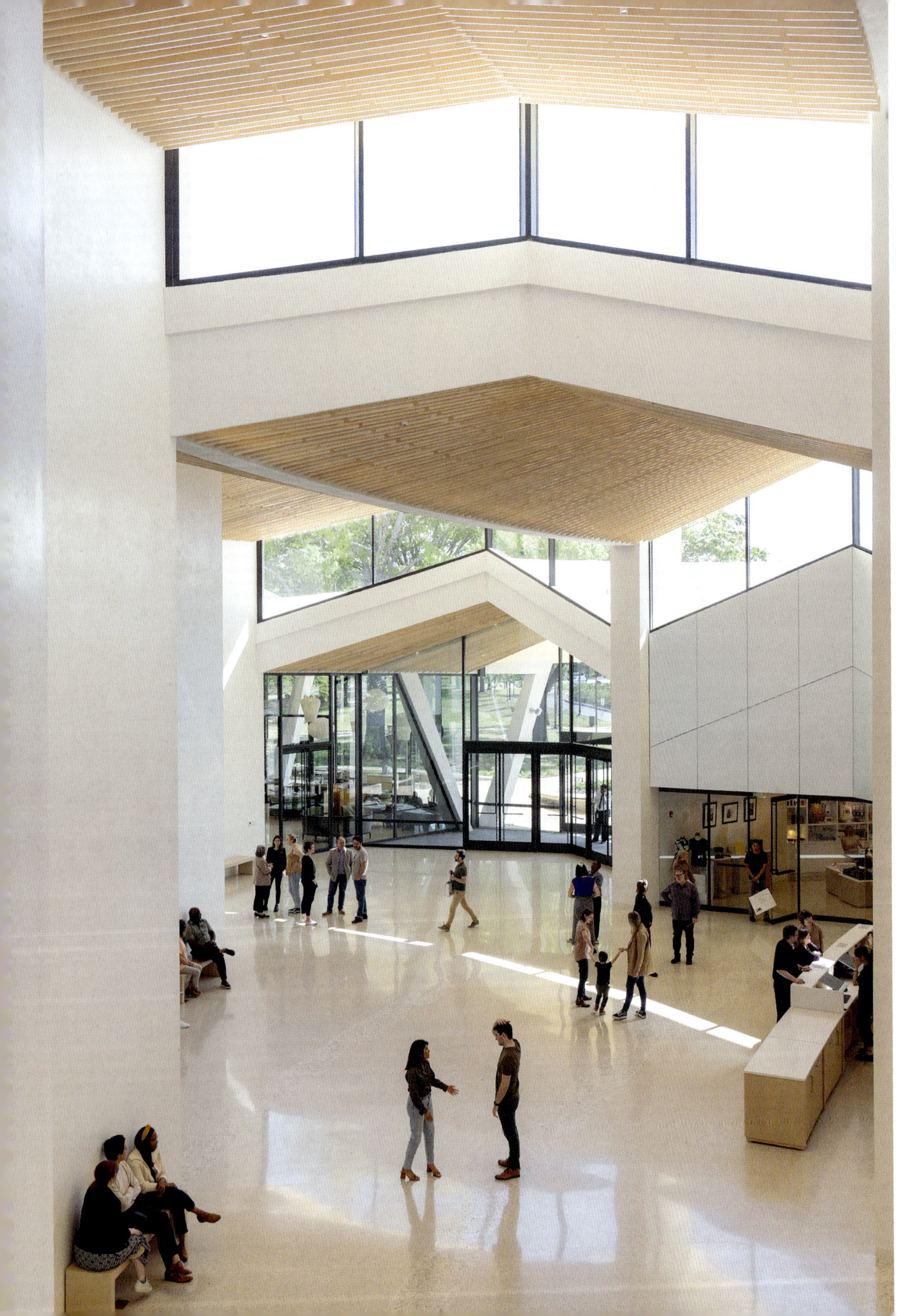

Stepping into the Museum, visitors enter the inviting, naturally lit Atrium, where they can see the entire space and choose a route to follow. The open design of the Atrium introduces visitors to the Museum's full range of offerings. From the Park Entrance at the south of the building, entry into each program space is clearly marked with a reflective or transparent portal. The softly curving walls and beams, along with the subtle finish lines in the floor, help guide visitors intuitively into these spaces and through the Atrium, creating a natural flow reinforced by the fluidly sculptural ceiling.

Clerestory windows fill the space with natural light and provide views of the park to the south. Materials and finishes—including the wood ceiling and staircase, polished plaster walls, custom concrete floor, and transparent or frosted glass—further accentuate the lightness of the space. Hidden hang points in the ceiling are designed to support suspended sculptures, expanding AMFA's ability to display large-format artwork outside the galleries.

The ceiling itself is a work of art that unfolds as visitors move through the Museum. Made of 6,000 individually suspended plywood slats, it imparts a sense of motion to the interior. While each slat is a straight, flat piece of wood arranged in a linear pattern, subtle differences in spacing and height create the illusion of sweeping curves and a flowing, undulating surface.

The Grand Staircase provides a smooth transition between the Museum's upper and lower levels and across the natural incline of the site. The wide and gently sloping staircase carries visitors upward to the Harriet and Warren Stephens Galleries and the Cultural Living Room on the second floor. Its white oak finish complements the wood ceiling.

Continuous Motion (2021), a redwood sculpture with a steel base by Robyn Horn, is on view at the base of the staircase. Using a chainsaw, power tools, and hand tools, Horn carved a single piece of wood into a form that suggests perpetual movement.

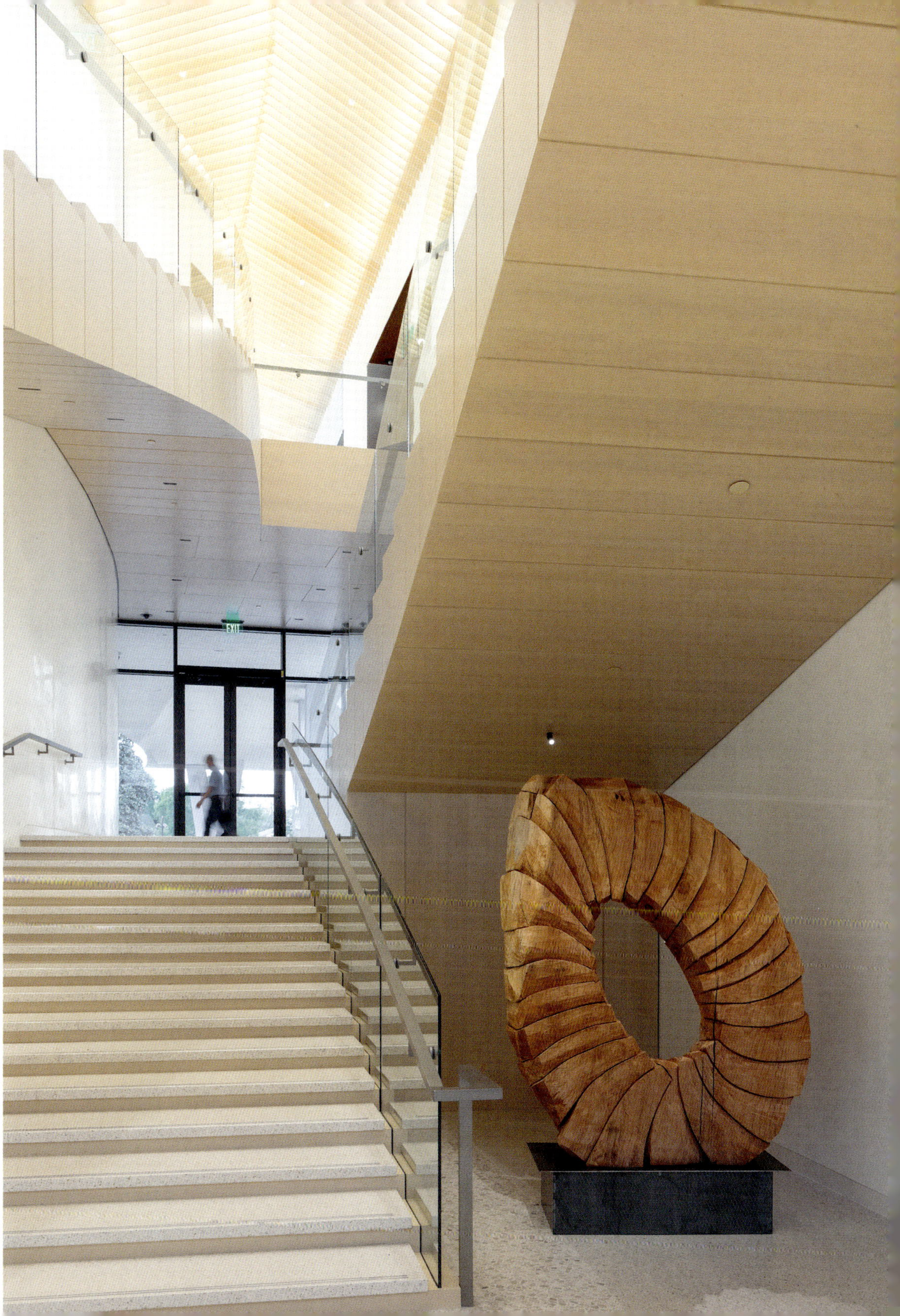

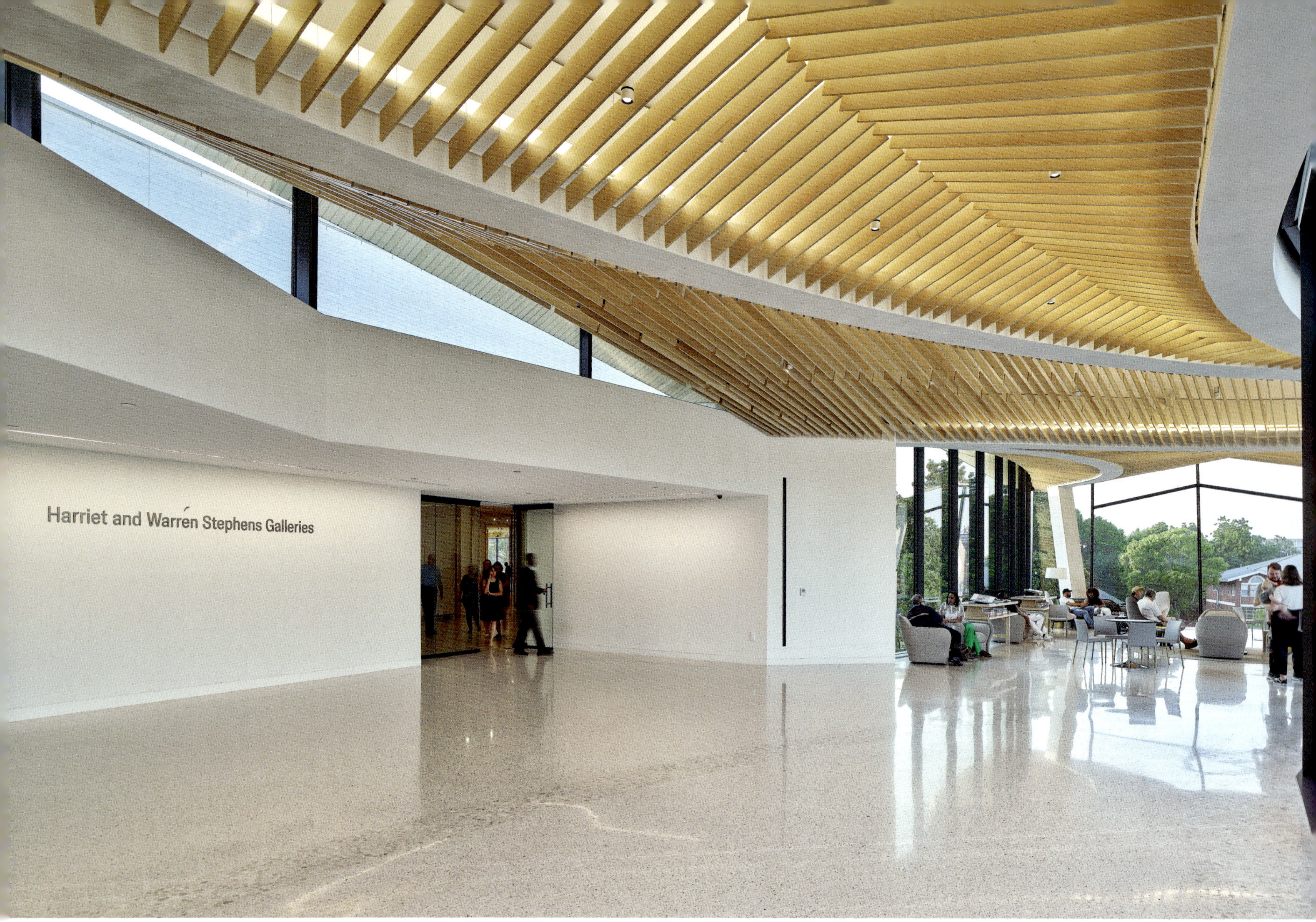

Located on the second level, the glass door entrance to the Harriet and Warren Stephens Galleries entices visitors by revealing works of art on display inside. Also visible is the diagonal enfilade, a series of galleries interconnected so that one space opens to the next. This architectural feature leads to the Art Perch, a window overlooking Ninth Street and the grounds outside. The Cultural Living Room, adjacent to the gallery entrance, offers visitors a peaceful space to gather or reflect on, and converse about, the art they have seen.

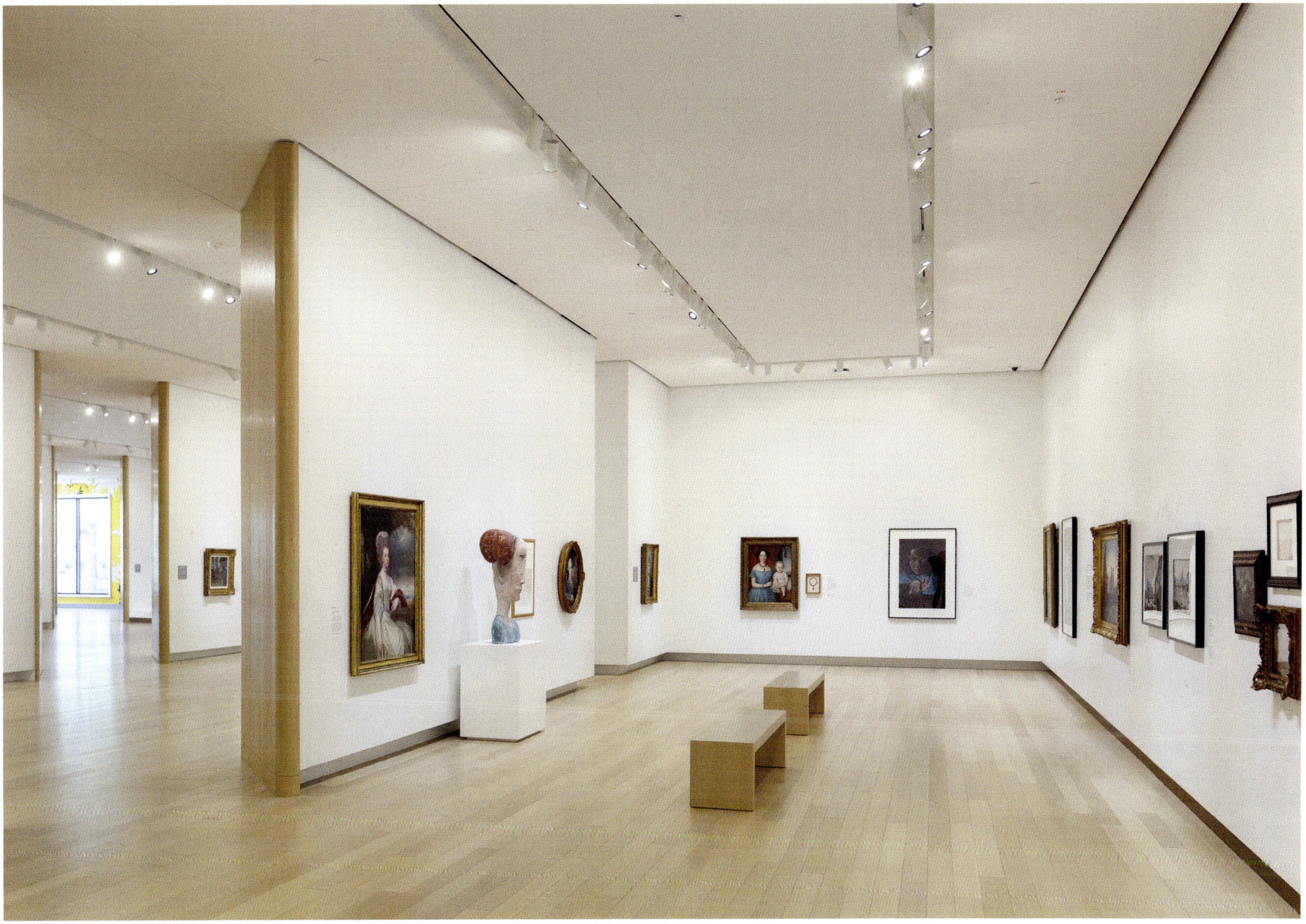

A series of five large spaces forms the galleries that showcase the AMFA Foundation's permanent collection. The innovative diagonal enfilade layout allows visitors to circulate with ease. The unique spatial arrangement also creates a strong sightline through all the galleries—providing views of different parts of the collection and encouraging visitors to discover new works, while orienting them to temporary installations at the large Art Perch window at the far end.

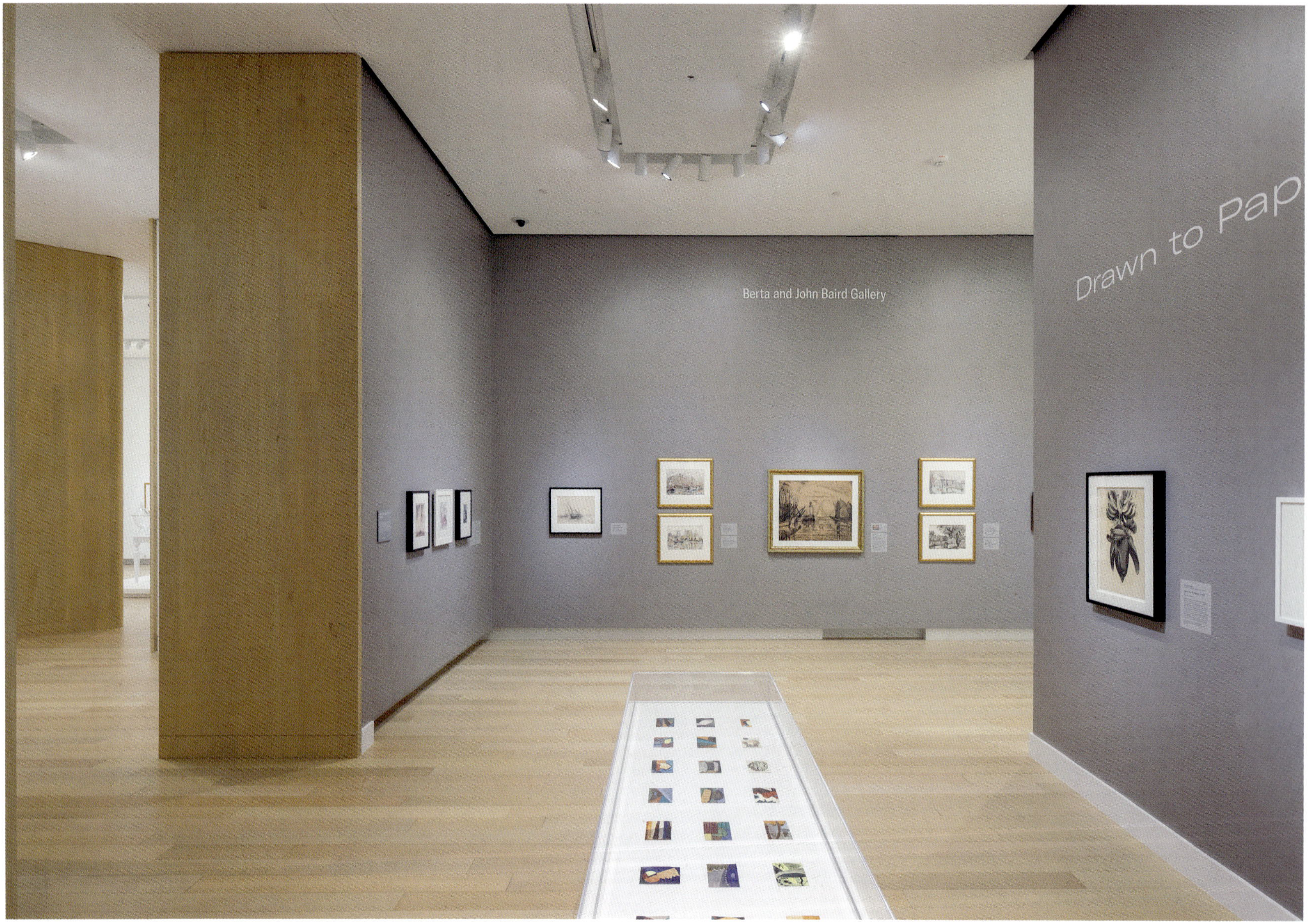

With their scale, refined materiality, and thoughtful detailing, the Harriet and Warren Stephens Galleries establish an elegant space for display of the collection and exhibitions. Mechanical vents and power outlets are hidden at the top and bottom of the walls, allowing visitors to focus on the artwork. White oak floors and wood casing bring natural warmth to the galleries.

This fresh space is supported by the existing columns and foundations of the Museum's former gallery wing. The conservation and reuse of these structural components makes an important contribution to the building's overall sustainability.

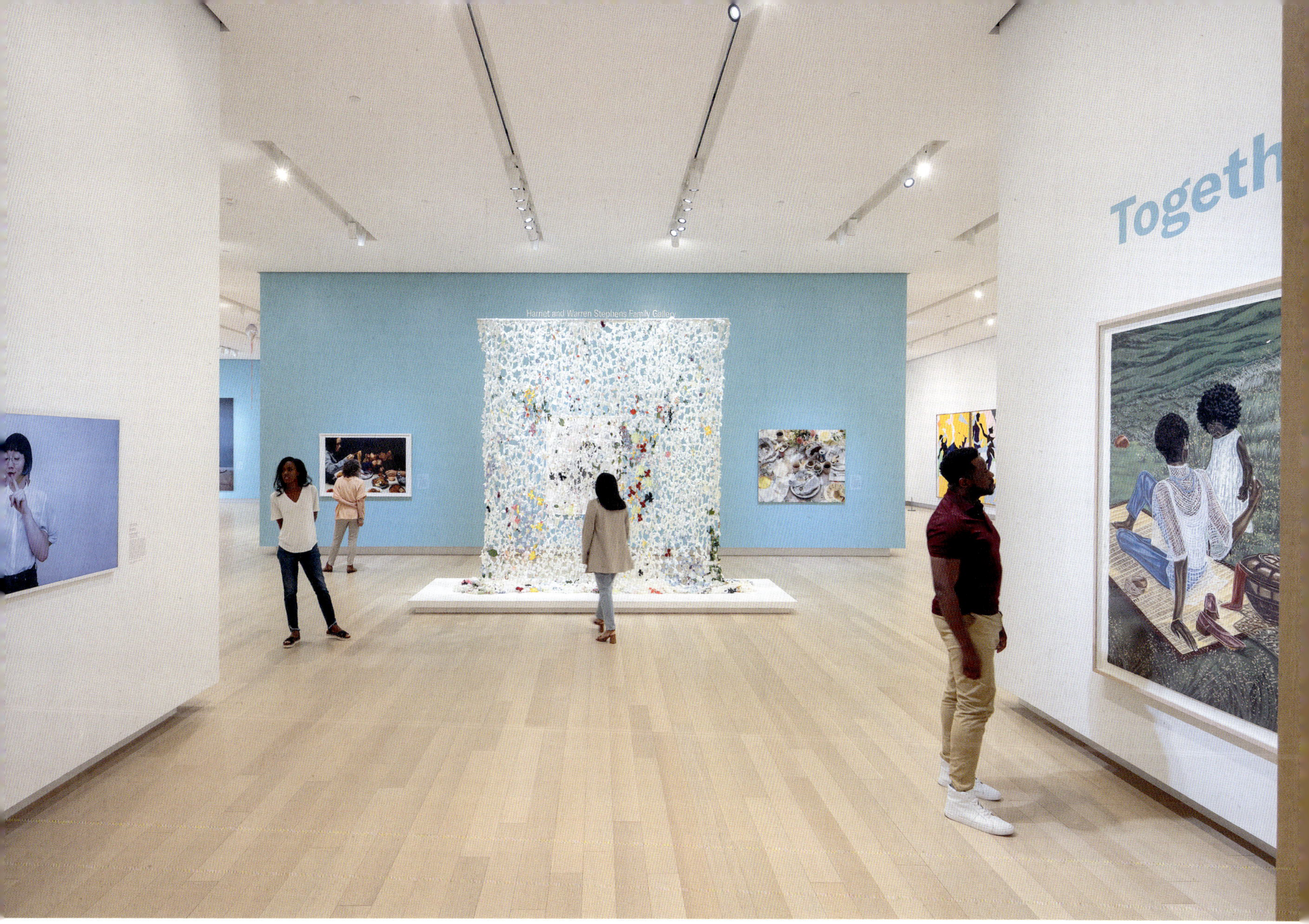

Comprising two large-scale, connected spaces, the Harriet and Warren Stephens Family Gallery displays special exhibitions. Its flexible design can accommodate a wide variety of works of art, spanning a range of formats, scales, and media.

Together, the inaugural exhibition in the Harriet and Warren Stephens Family Gallery, celebrates community, friends, family, and humanity's connection to the natural world. Presenting contemporary artworks in varying media by artists from wide-ranging backgrounds, *Together* represents the diversity and creativity to be found in future exhibitions presented at AMFA.

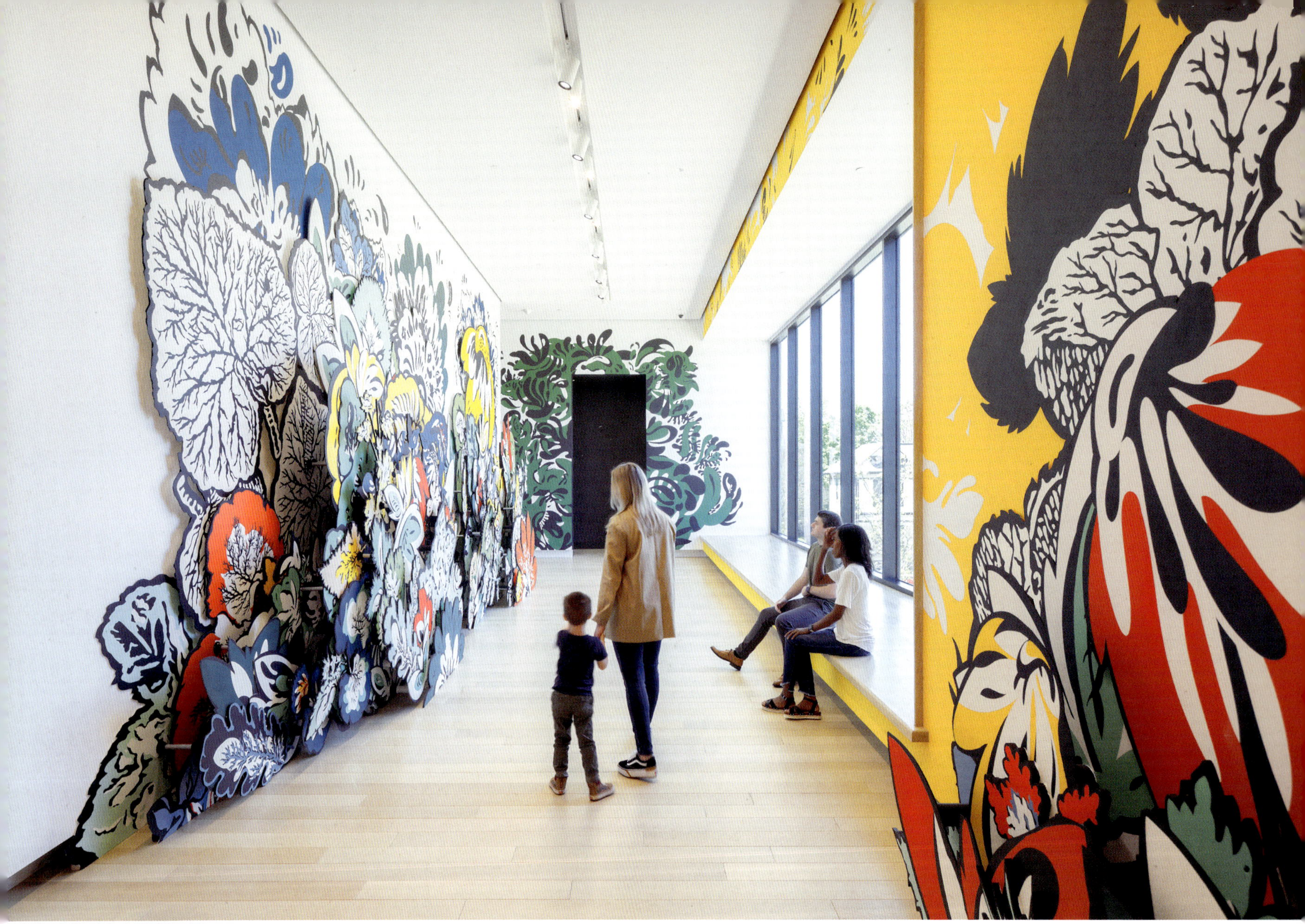

When visitors reach the northernmost corner of the permanent collection galleries, they discover a delightful surprise: an expansive view of the outdoors. The large window and built-in bench of the Art Perch provide visitors with a comfortable place in which to pause and consider site-specific installations on the adjacent walls or look out onto the landscape and neighborhood beyond. Providing a rejuvenating moment of natural light within the galleries, the space features a freestanding wall designed to prevent sunlight from damaging permanent collection works in the adjacent Jackson T. Stephens Gallery.

Artist Natasha Bowdoin created the inaugural Art Perch installation, *Spring Song* (2022–2023). With its graphic lines and high-contrast palette, Bowdoin's gardenscape dazzles the eye from afar—pedestrians and motorists traveling down Ninth Street may view her work through the 32-foot-long window.

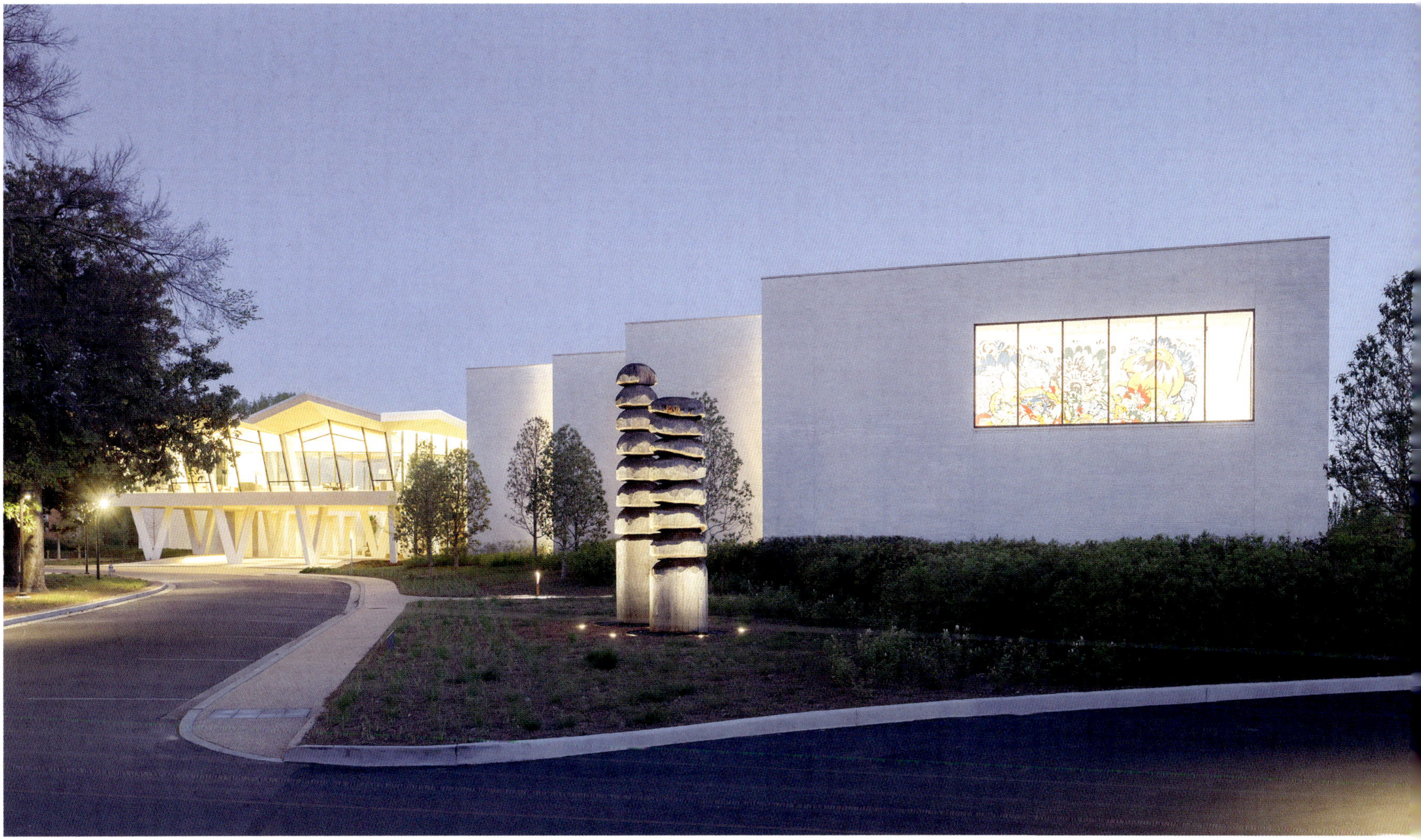

From the outside, the Art Perch's large window provides a framed view of featured artworks inside, catching the eyes of visitors and passersby and inviting them in. Running alongside an arced path to the Courtyard Entrance, a diverse understory of native grasses and perennials softens the edge of the drive. *Two Columns* (2004), by David Nash, a sculpture of carved and burned redwood, rises among the plants. Native trees such as wax myrtles, oaks, and magnolias are incorporated throughout the landscape.

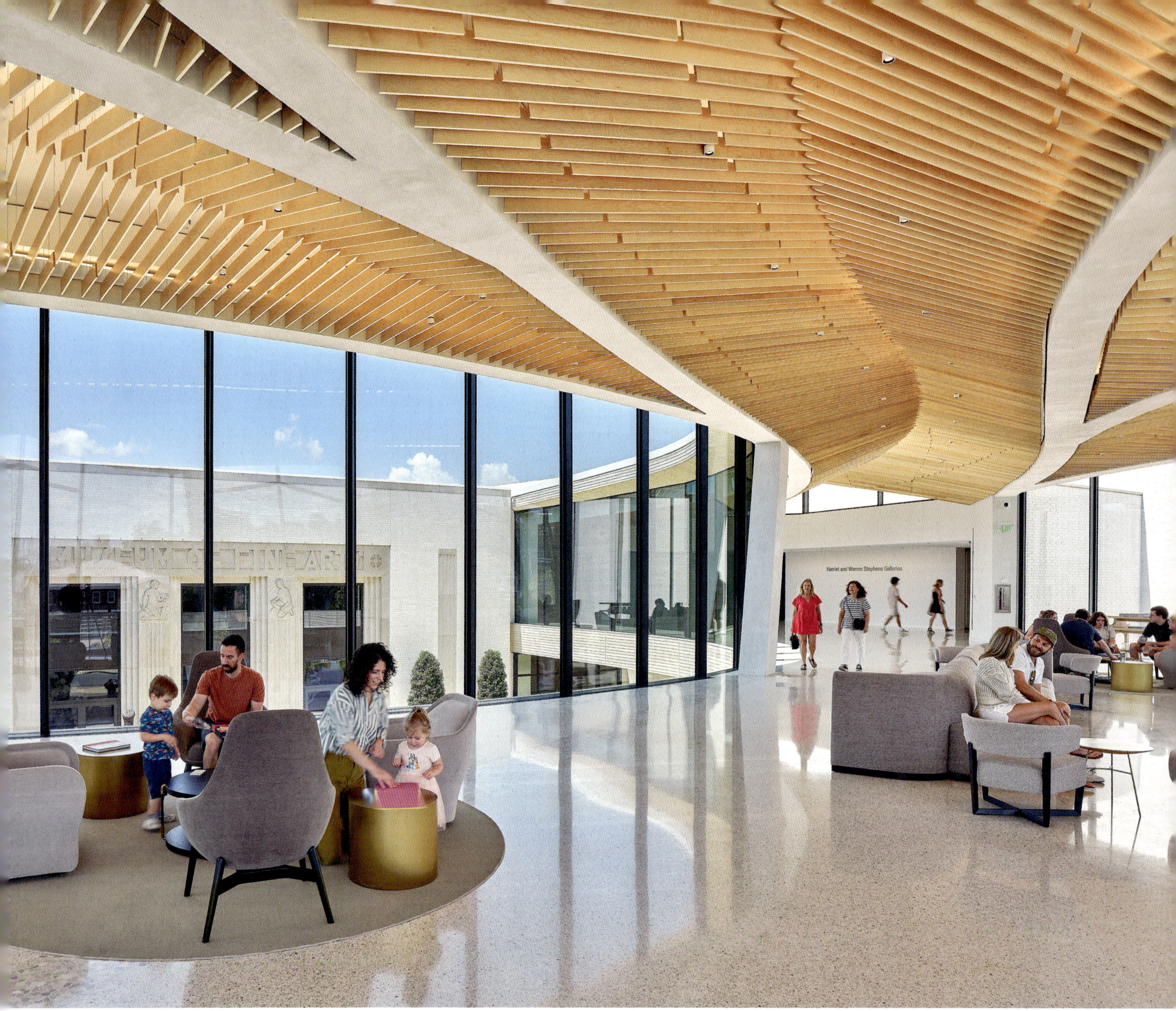
Harriet and Warren Stephens Galleries

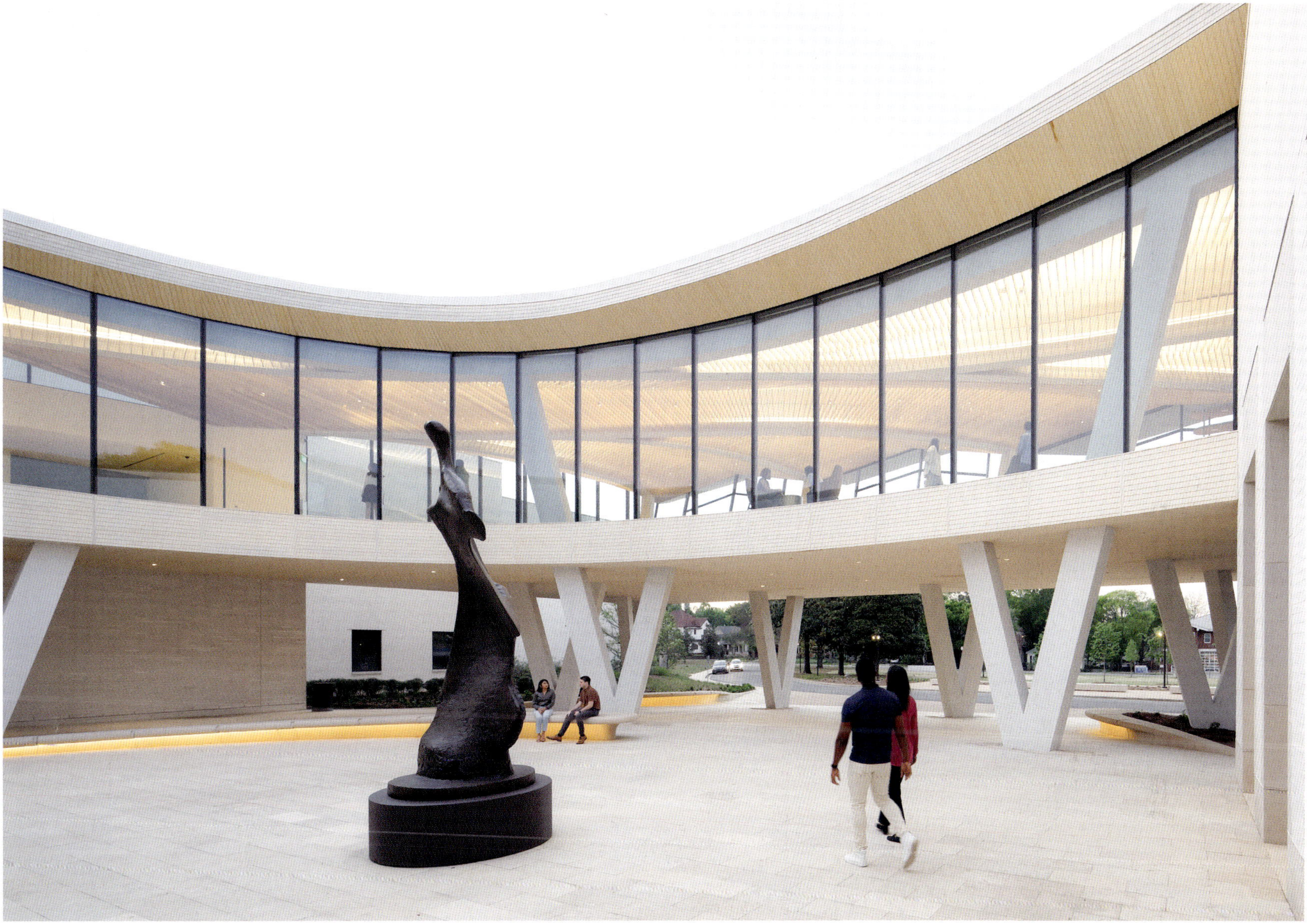

Entering the Cultural Living Room evokes a feeling of lightness. Its transparent, angled façade provides a panoramic view of the surrounding park and a sense of floating above the grounds. Below the undulating wood ceiling, which rises to meet the building's column structure, visitors can relax on comfortable lounge seating and discuss or reflect on the art they have just seen. The space is also free and open to the public for gathering, and its flexible furniture can be rearranged to accommodate various events and programs.

Combining dramatic design with cozy seating, the Cultural Living Room is a social beacon attracting vibrant activity from the Museum and the entire Little Rock community. The curving lines of the Cultural Living Room's exterior create a striking backdrop for Henry Moore's *Large Standing Figure: Knife Edge* (1961, cast in 1976), on display in the Courtyard.

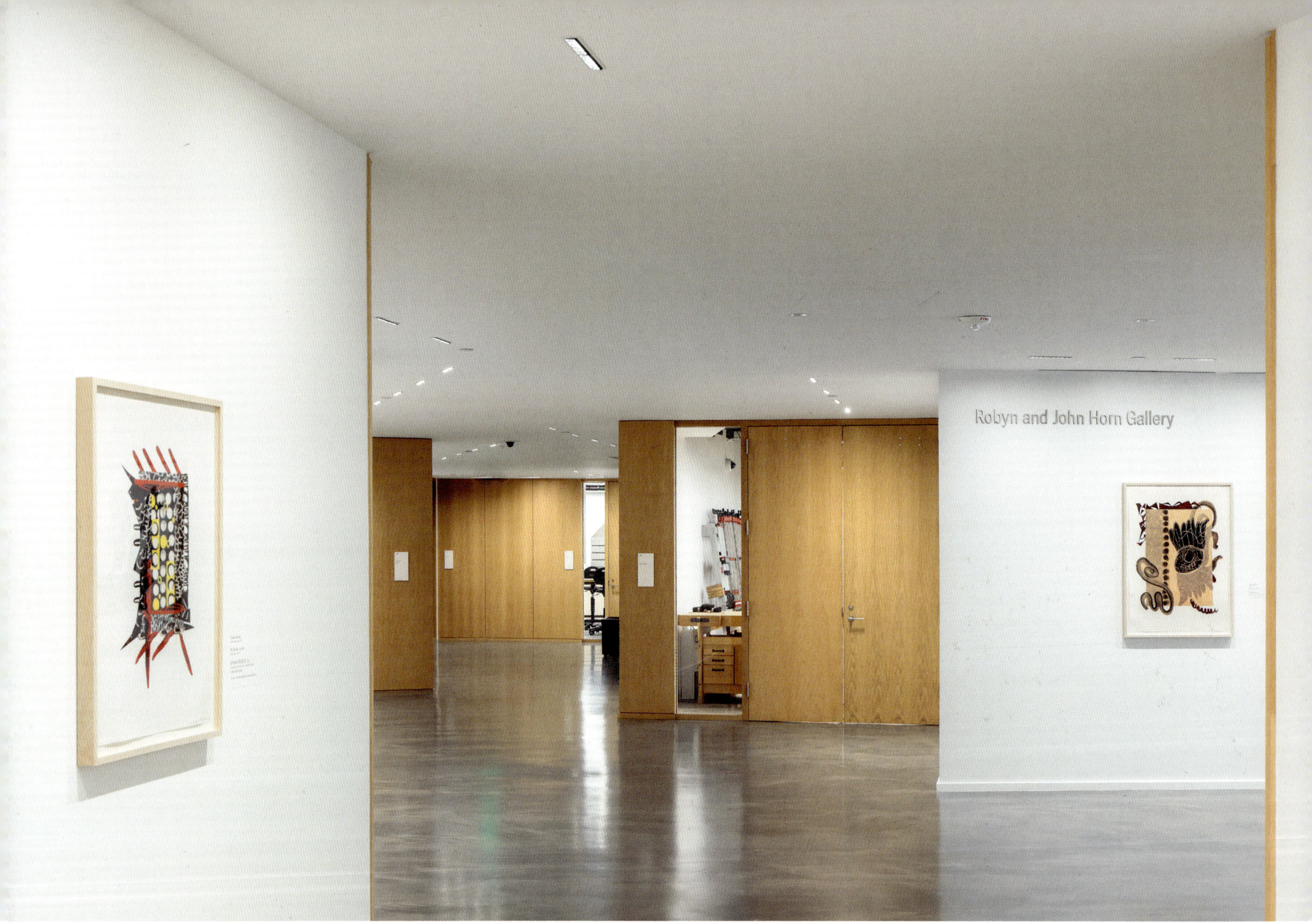

The Robyn and John Horn Gallery creates an exciting point of arrival for the Windgate Art School. Echoing the design intent and visitor experience of the Museum's Atrium, this space immediately orients students by revealing glimpses and clear entries into the different classroom studios. The Gallery also presents temporary exhibitions and serves as a place for Art School students and teachers to interact before and after class. Inaugurating the Horn Gallery, *Chakaia Booker: Intentional Risks* presents one sculpture and 20 prints made by Booker in collaboration with master printers at the Robert Blackburn Printmaking Workshop in New York. The artist uses chine collé, a process in which tissue-thin paper is adhered to a thicker support paper through the weight of the printing press. Blackburn, who established his workshop in 1947, gave a printmaking demonstration at the Art School in February 1985.

Windgate Art School includes eight classroom studios, where students of all ages can learn drawing, painting, ceramics, glass, metals, woodworking, printmaking, and other media. The ceramics studio offers classes and workshops in hand building and wheel throwing clay.

In all the classroom studios, custom Baltic birch millwork and burnished concrete floors create inviting yet robust spaces for making and learning.

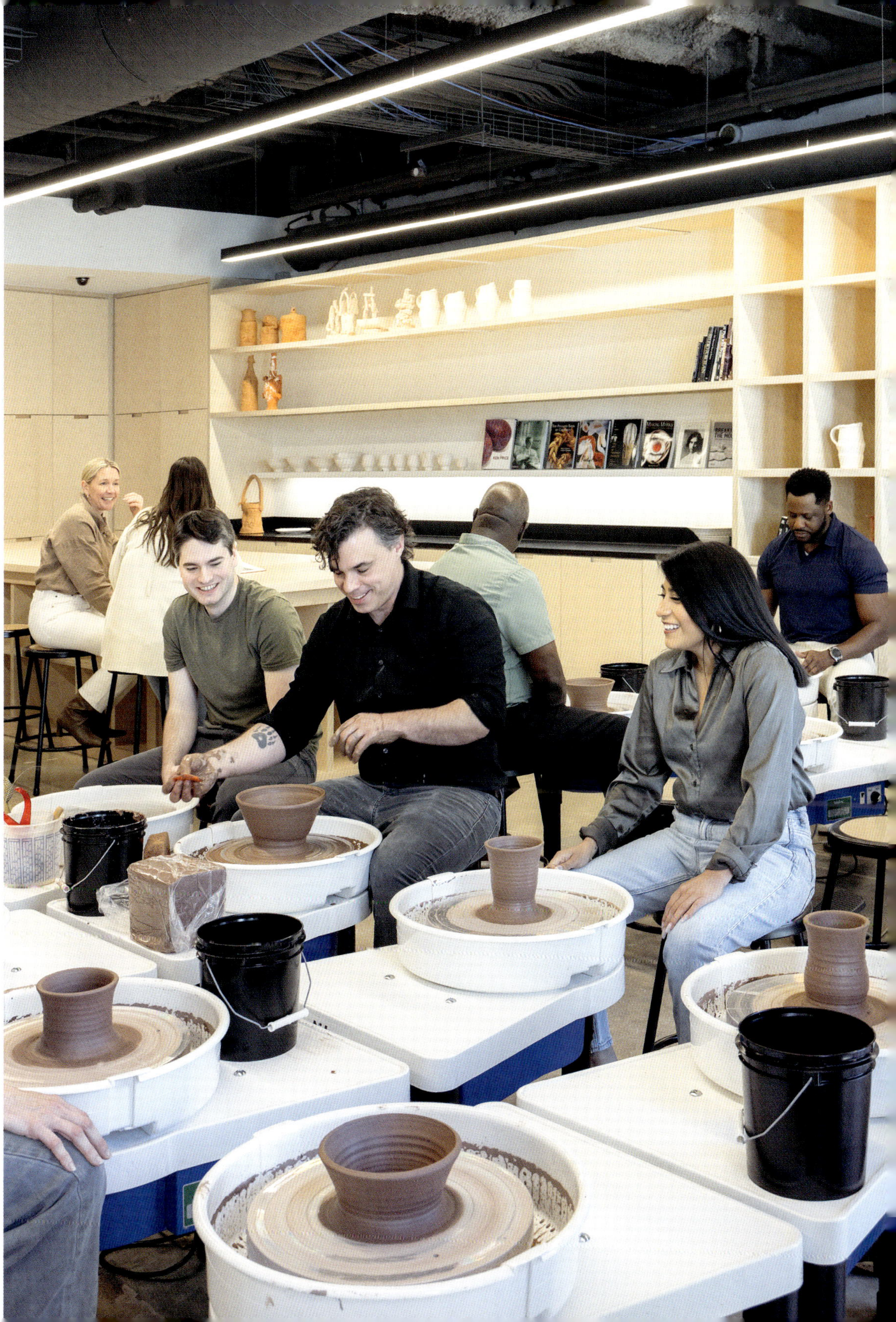

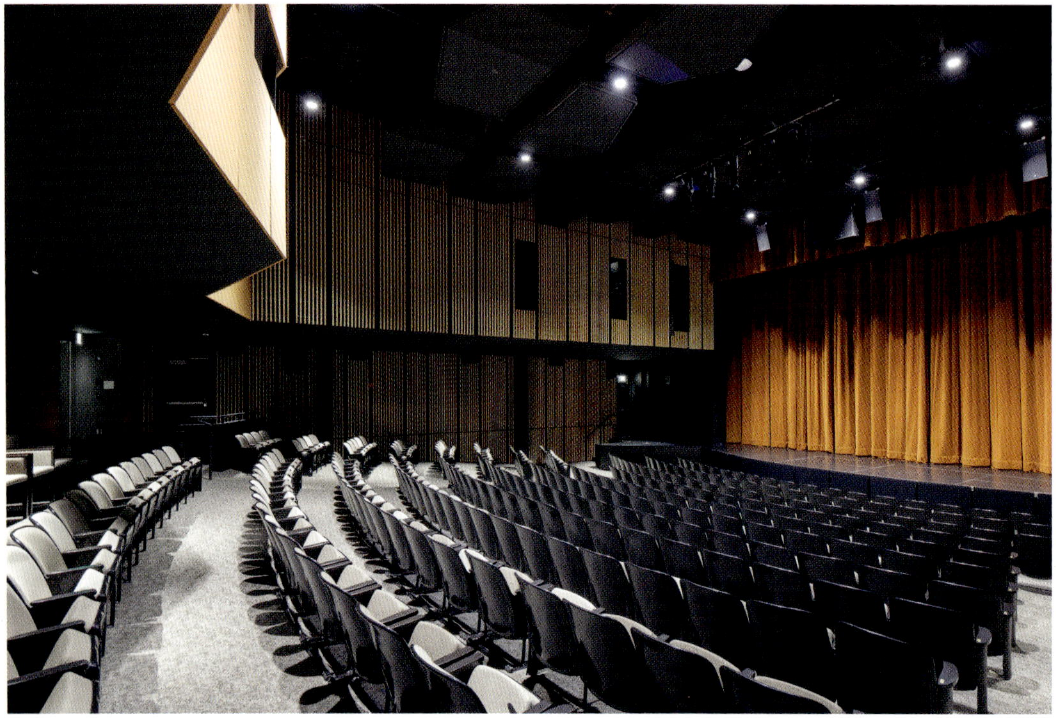

In the 350-seat Performing Arts Theater, many of the original 1960s design elements have been preserved and restored, including the shell, the stage, the seats, and the faceted acoustic reflectors, maintaining the unique character of the space for new generations. A complete technical overhaul using state-of-the-art equipment and technologies allows AMFA to host a broader spectrum of performances than before. New slatted-wood paneling provides an improved acoustic and aesthetic environment, and the Theater's reconfigured seating layout improves accessibility for all guests.

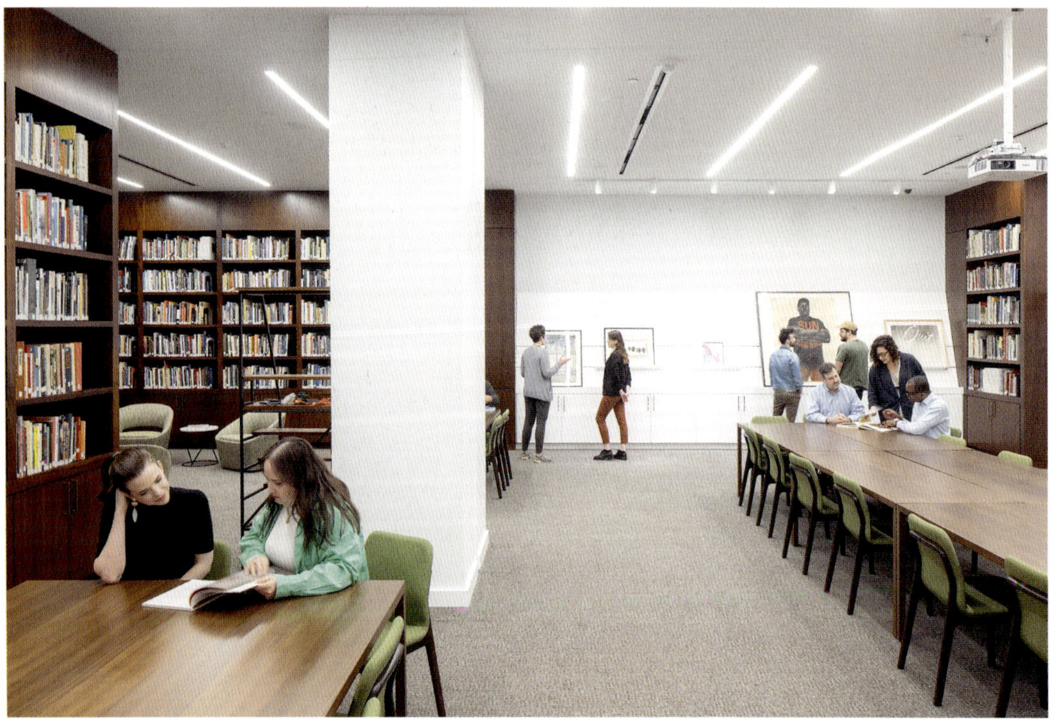

The stately Terri and Chuck Erwin Collections Resource Center is designed for formal meetings and presentations, study of the AMFA Foundation Collection, and other activities and gatherings requiring a quieter, more intimate setting. Because all of the AMFA Foundation's permanent collection cannot always be on view, this space allows visitors and scholars to examine selected works up close. Built-in ledges accommodate art viewing, and custom walnut millwork houses the Museum's book collection.

When visitors enter the Museum from the Courtyard Entrance through the 1937 façade, they find themselves in a new Lobby inspired by the Art Deco qualities of the original Museum of Fine Arts. The Lobby's three sets of tall glass doors frame views of the central greeter desk and second-floor mezzanine, the new volume of which echoes the grand proportions of the 1937 façade openings. Compositions of walnut paneling emphasize the sense of verticality in the space and celebrate the craftsmanship of its makers, both hallmarks of Art Deco architecture.

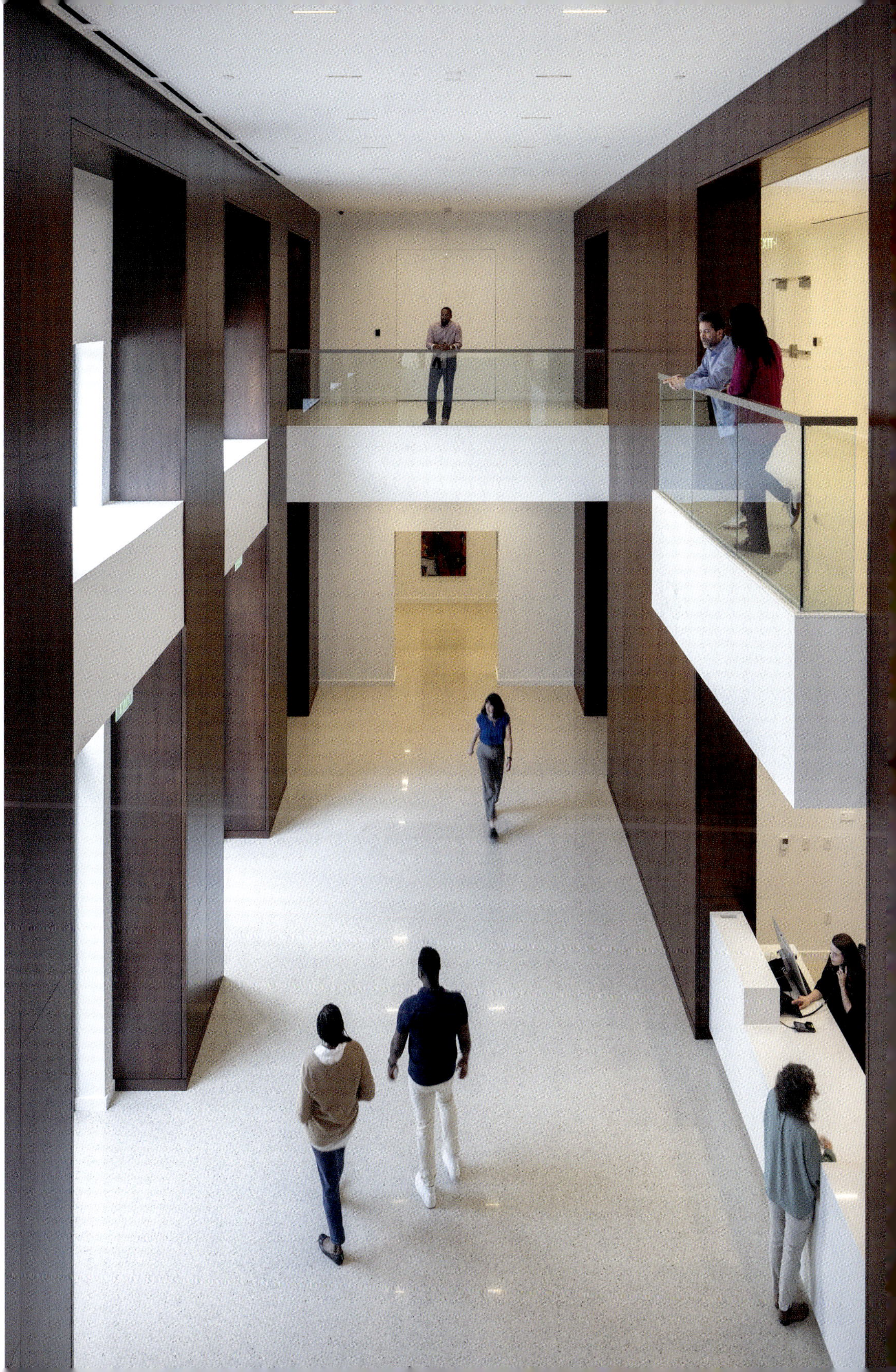

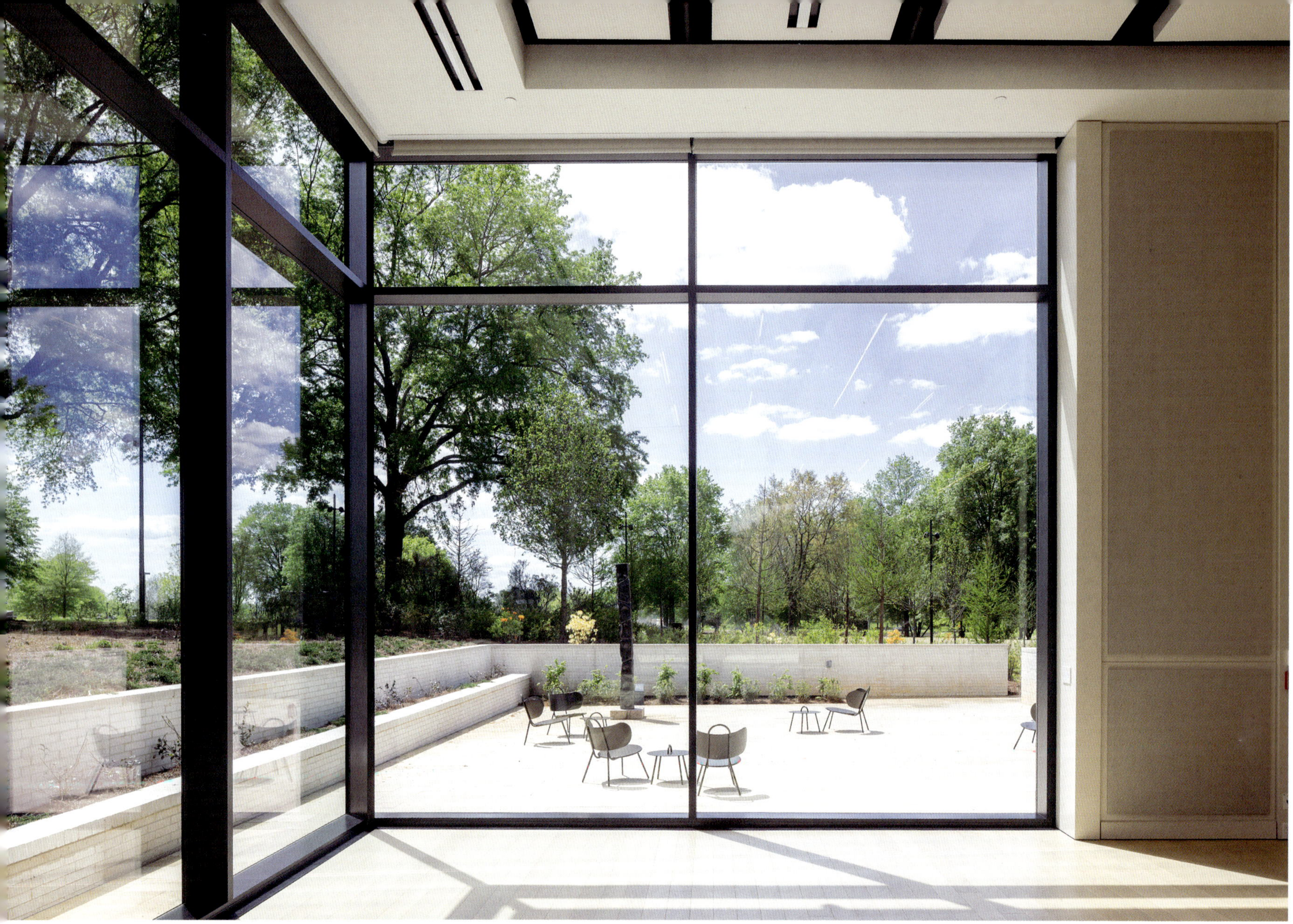

The Glass Box is a flexible event space that embraces its surroundings. Capable of hosting a wide spectrum of programs, including lectures and performances, the room is conceived as a burst of daylight and energy. Floor-to-ceiling glass makes the space transparent and full of natural light, while continuous mirrors along its north side reflect the landscape back into the room.

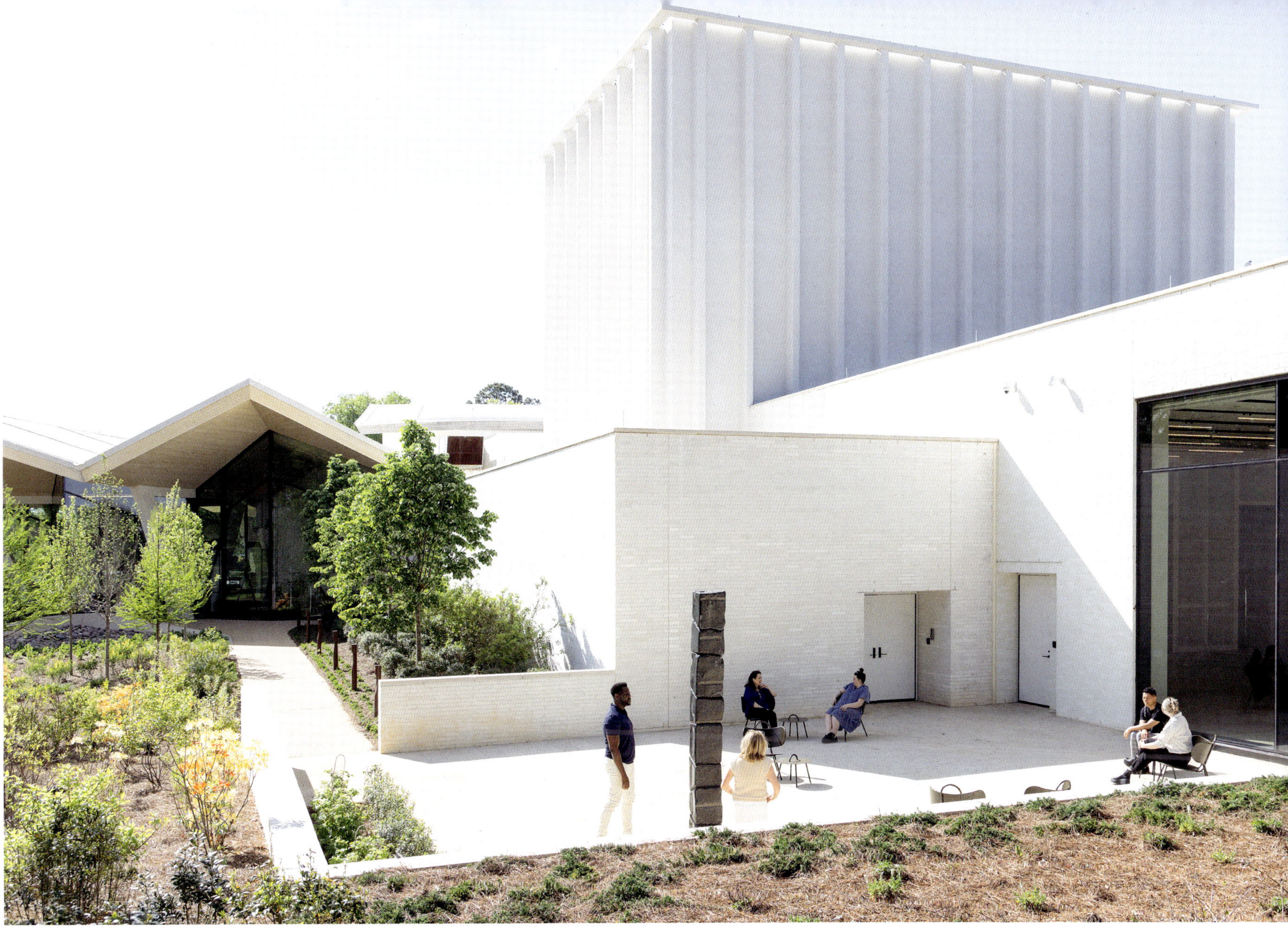

The Glass Box provides views of the historic parade grounds of MacArthur Park as well as the new Event Lawn and biodiverse garden landscape. Activities taking place inside can spill outdoors onto the connected Glass Box Terrace, which is surrounded by softscape plantings, benches, and ambient lighting for evening events. A black-and-pink granite sculpture, *Broken Earth* (2003), by the artist Jesús Moroles, was expressly chosen to lend a formal artistic character to the outdoor space.

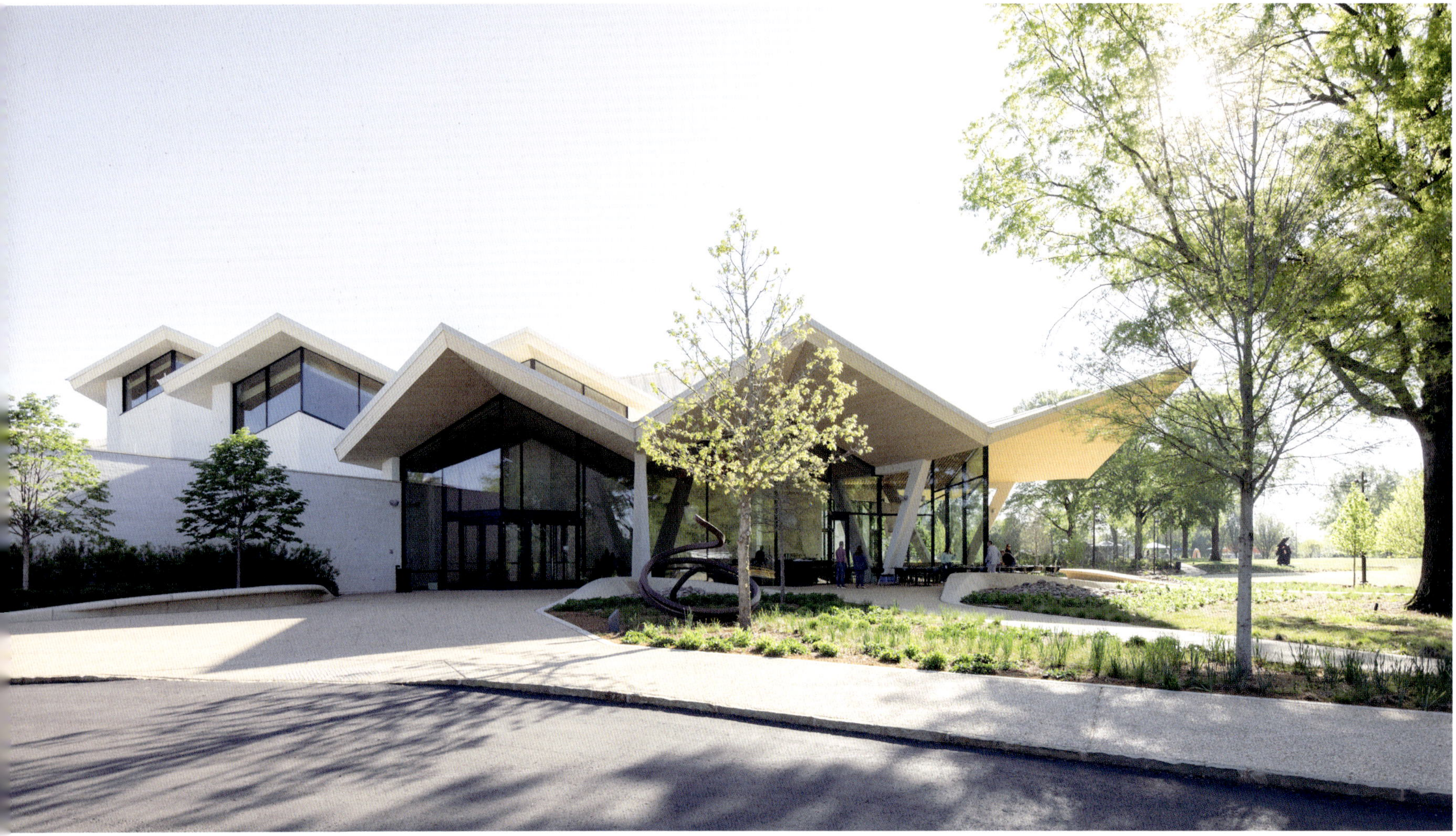

At the south end of the Museum, the building's central stem emerges outward to form another entrance, this one oriented toward MacArthur Park. More informal than its counterpart to the north, the Park Entrance steps down in height, along with the site's topography, to meet visitors. The deep overhangs of the folded-plate roof create a sheltered dining terrace for the new indoor-outdoor Park Grill restaurant. Here, visitors, diners, and community members can socialize, relax, and enjoy the revitalized landscape.

In addition to providing shade and improving the building's energy performance, the roof's pleats are also designed to direct rainwater into the gardens next to the building. These rain gardens capture and filter the water before distributing it throughout the MacArthur Park landscape and, eventually, into Foster Pond at the south end of the site.

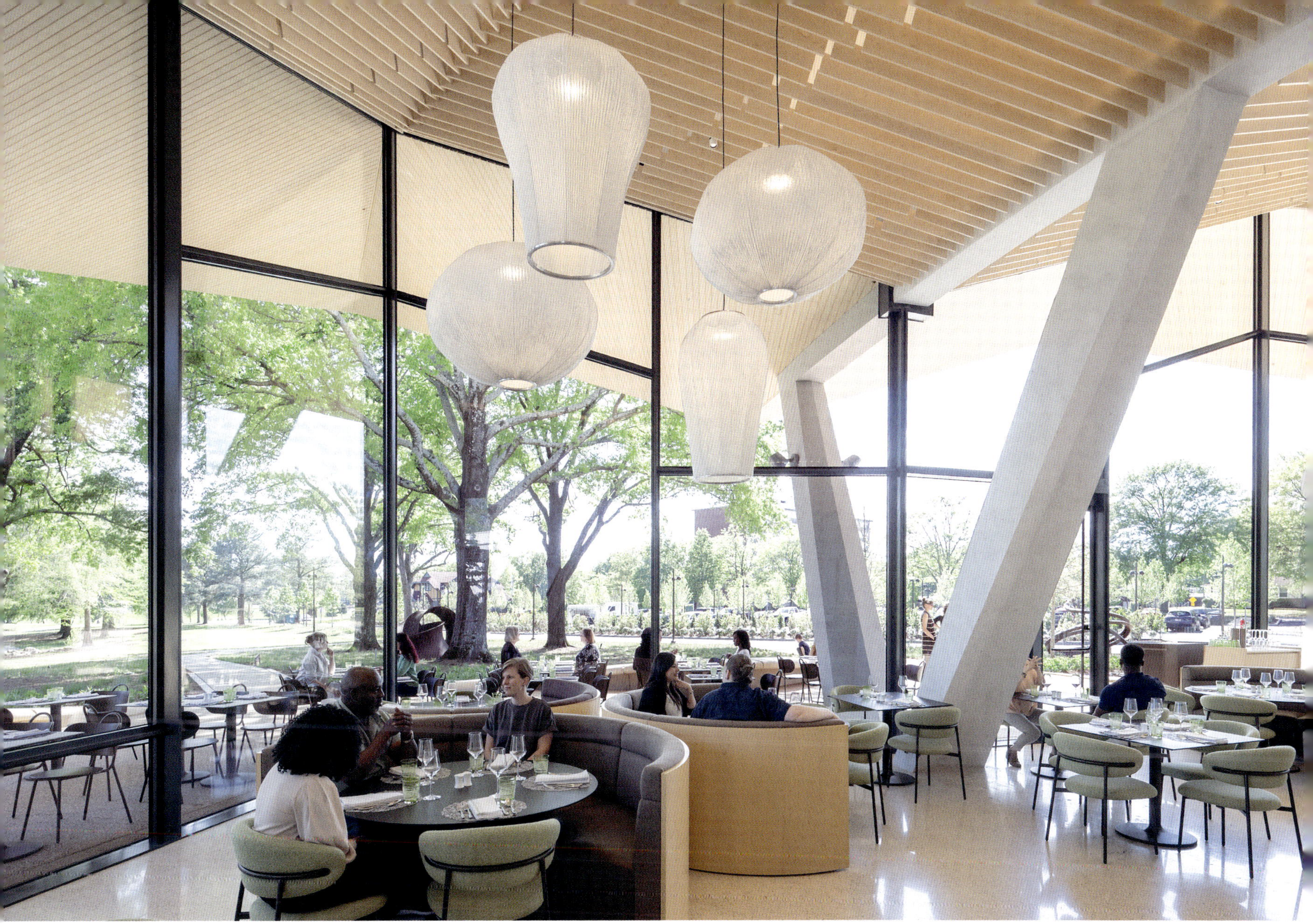

Animating the south end of the Museum, the Park Grill restaurant complements the Museum's cultural and educational offerings, providing new opportunities for socializing and relaxing. Inside, the full-height glass walls connect diners with the new gardens and sculptures outdoors.

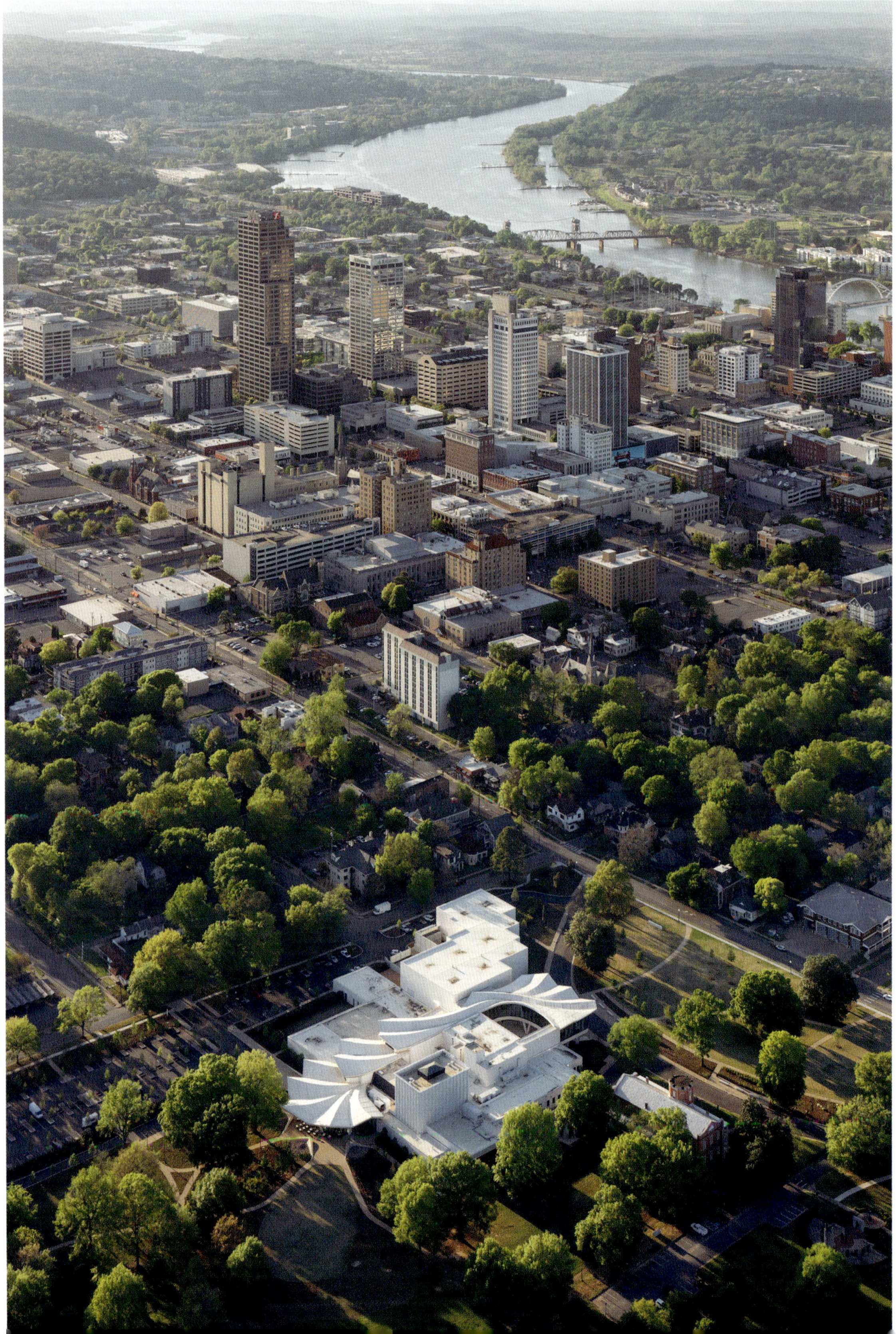

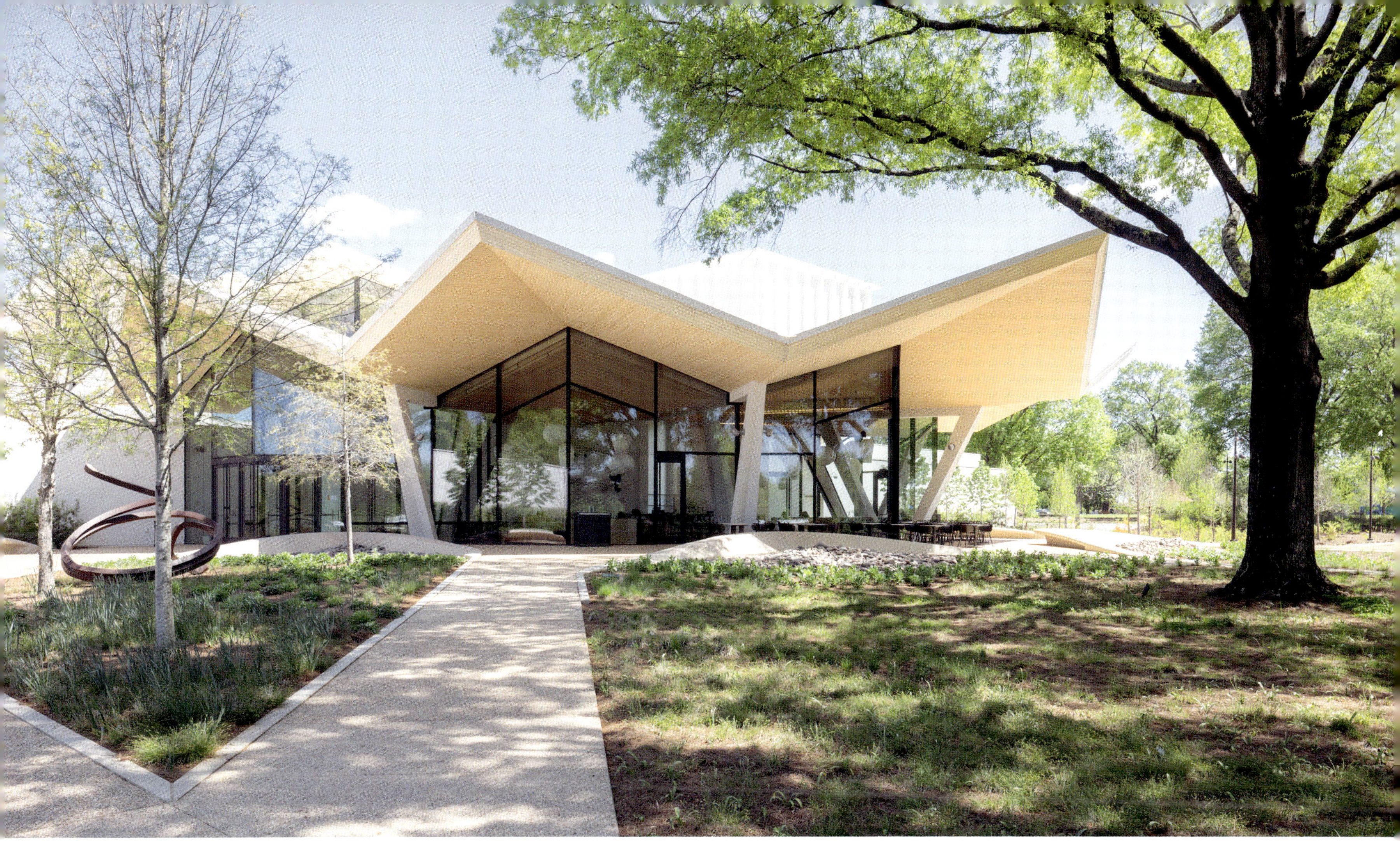

Architecture and landscape are intrinsically linked in the transformed Museum. From the earliest stages of design, Studio Gang and SCAPE worked with the Museum to craft the experience of a true "museum in a park," nesting the building within a framework of more than 250 newly planted native trees that are designed to merge with the existing canopy over time.

The central architectural gesture of the folded-plate roof extends outward into MacArthur Park in new, petal-shaped stormwater gardens that collect rainwater runoff from the roof. These gardens incorporate native stone features and plants found in landscapes across rural Arkansas, from the foothills of the Ouachita Mountains to low, grassy oak savannas to the northeast.

The Museum's new walking paths encourage visitors to meander through the park and AMFA's outdoor installations. They also connect the surrounding community with the Museum, physically as well as visually.

At the south, the paths that branch off from the restaurant terrace continue the flowing perimeter lines of the pleated roof. At the top of each petal garden, a curving bench made of precast concrete provides a comfortable place to rest at the edge of the terrace. *Indeterminate Line* (1994), a rolled steel sculpture by Bernar Venet, loops up from the ground, echoing the curved form of the concrete benches.

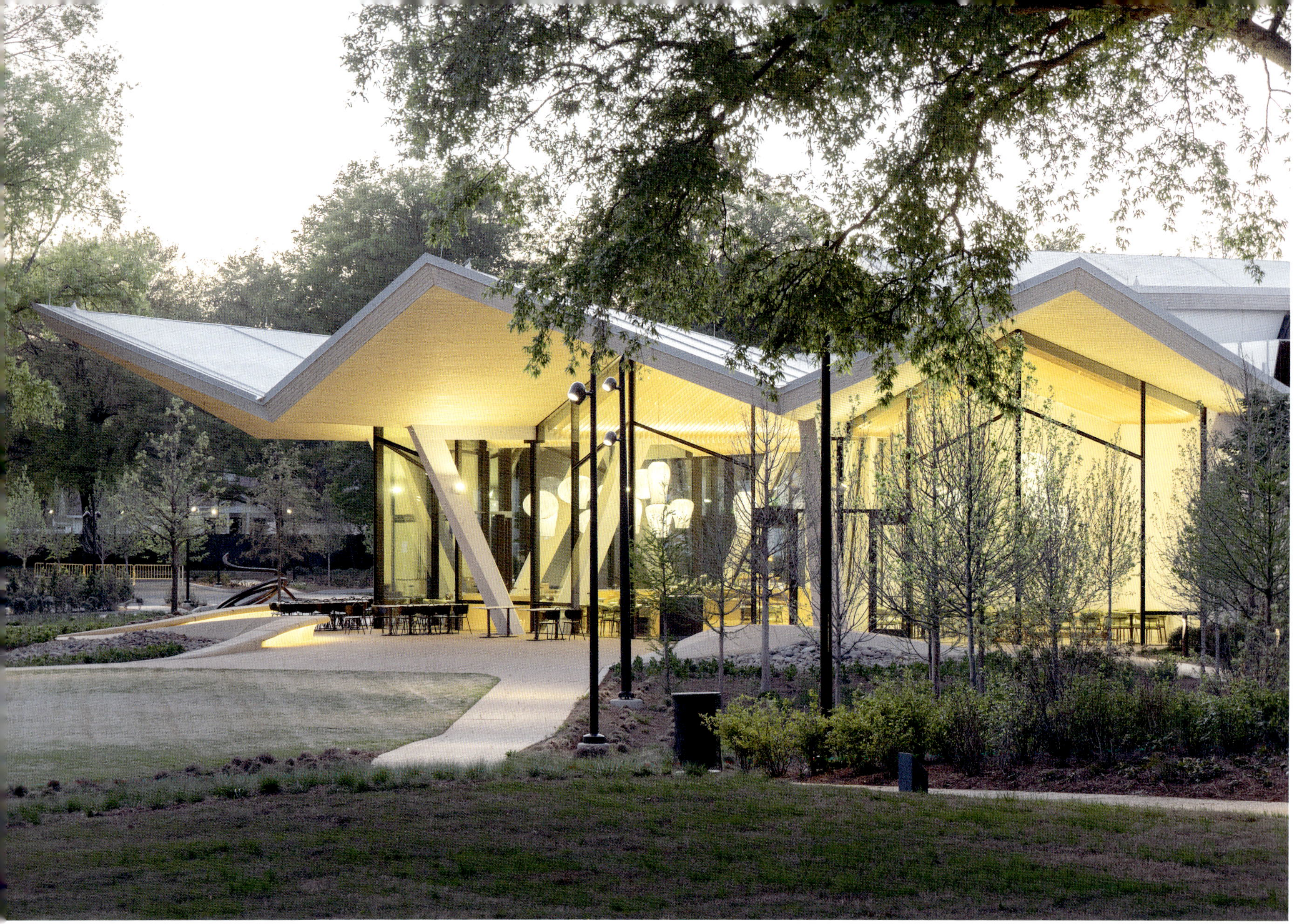

Located off the restaurant at the south of the Museum campus, the Event Lawn is designed for hosting AMFA activities and special events. This open, flexibly programmed green space is framed by walking paths and newly landscaped native plants and trees, with MacArthur Park as a backdrop. The Museum incorporates high-performance lawn design across its landscapes, including free-draining, expanded-shale, and sand-blended soils that drain more efficiently during periods of heavy rain.

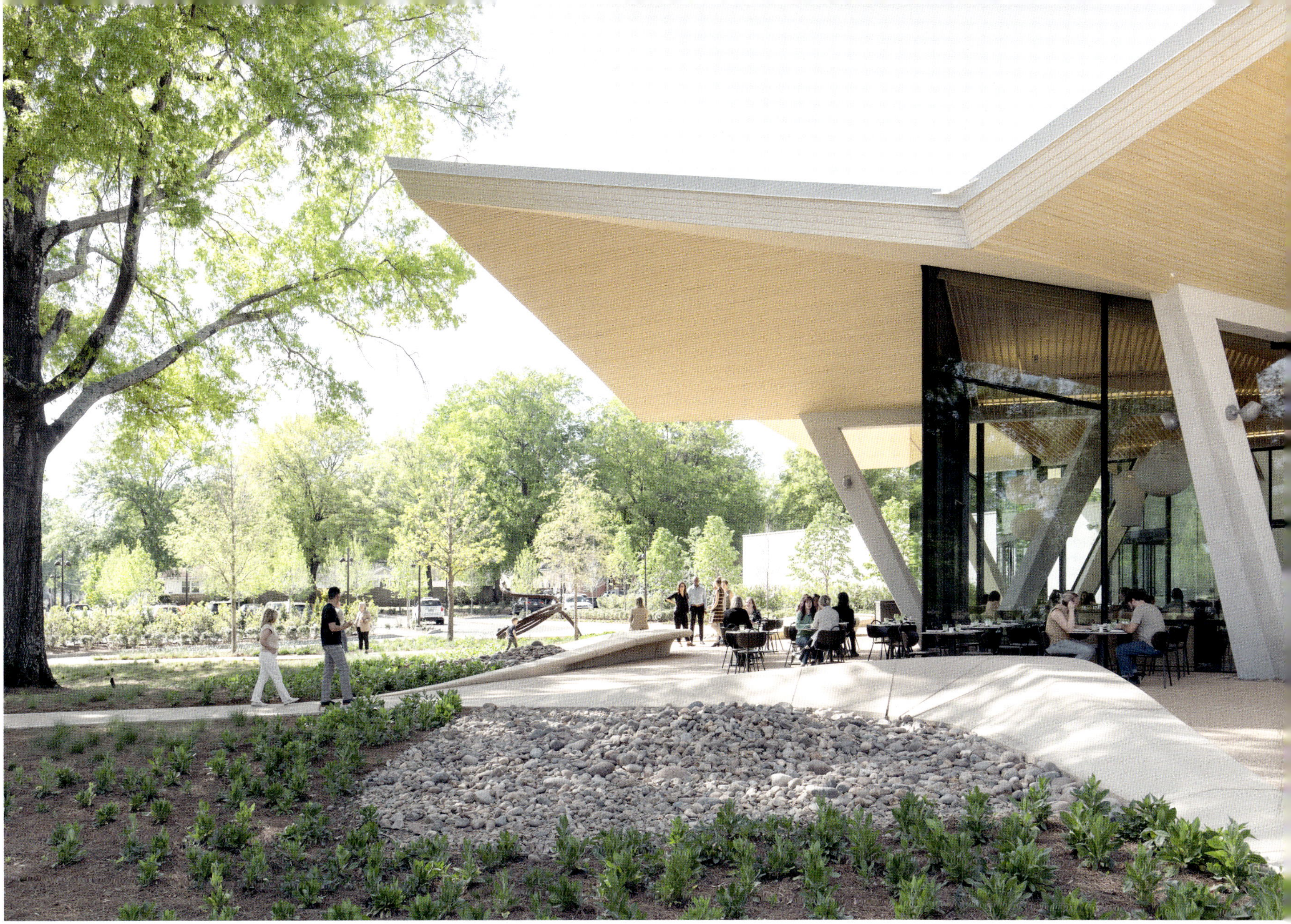

Planted groves along the west side of the building create an immersive, forested edge for the Museum campus that blends outward into the park. The landscape design intentionally preserves the existing robust oak canopy and incorporates a matrix of new oaks that will gradually merge with the historic canopy. Their combined foliage provides shade and beauty for the Museum's expanded outdoor spaces. Ecologically, the additional oaks allow a greater diversity of ground cover, birds, and insects to thrive on the Museum grounds, fostering a verdant habitat that visitors and the public can enjoy throughout the seasons. The sculptural gardens in the foreground receive rainwater from the Museum's roof and channel it into the landscape beyond.

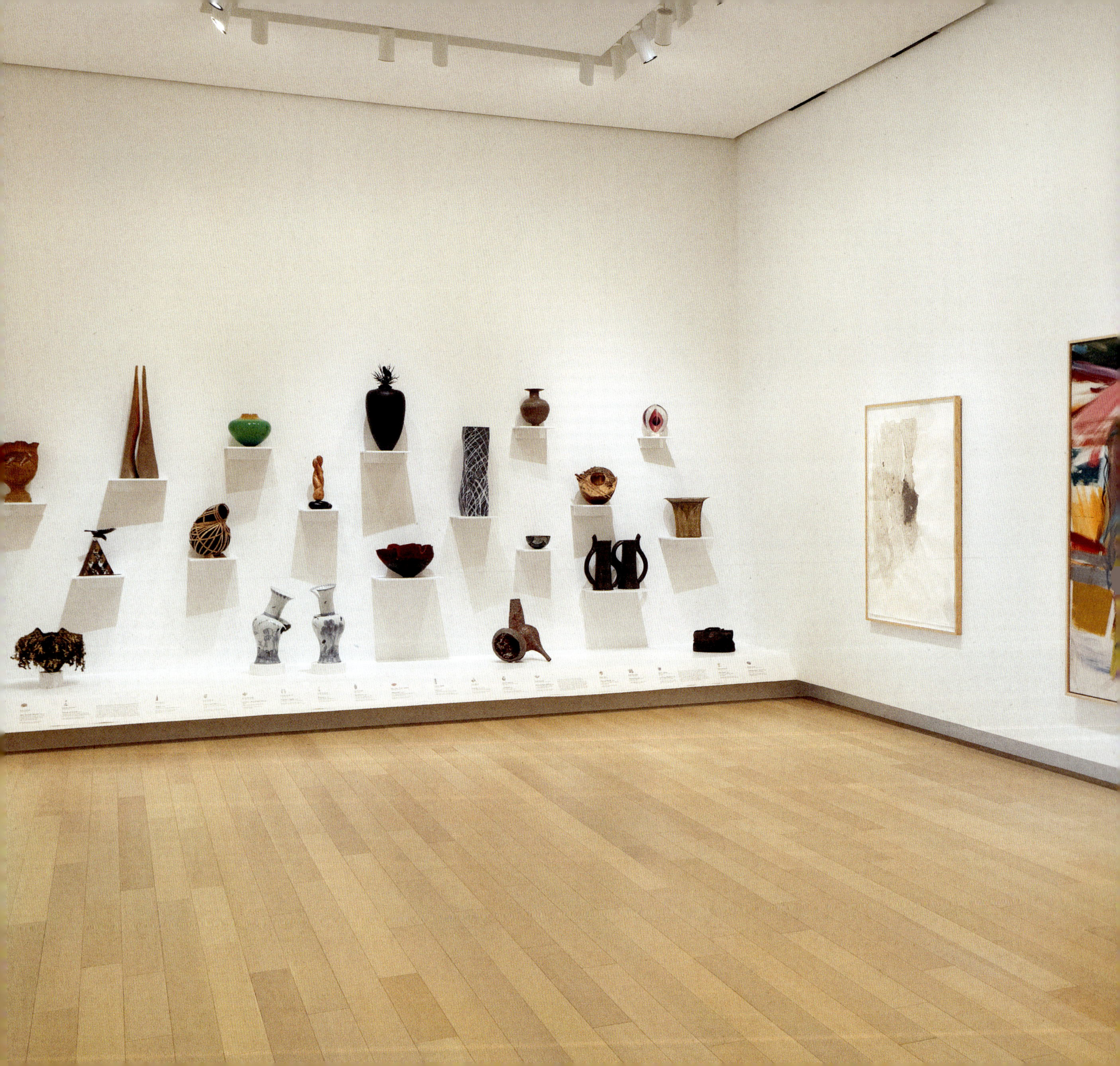

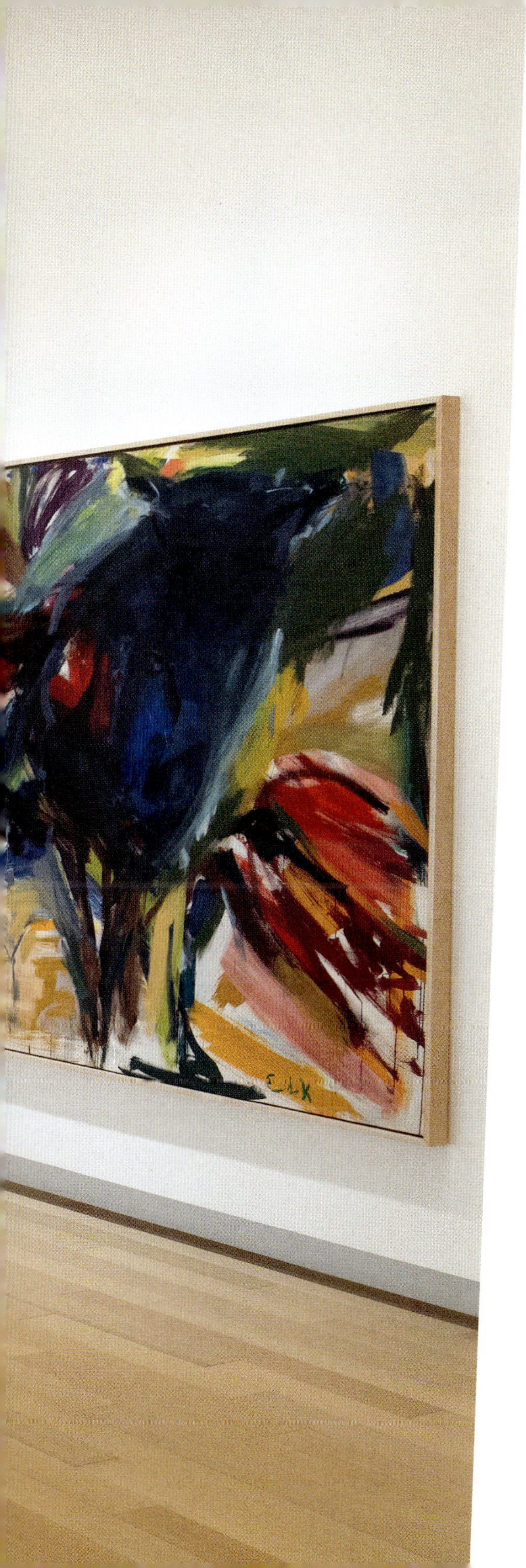

A Museum Reimagined

Dr. Victoria Ramirez, Executive Director, Arkansas Museum of Fine Arts

Arkansas Museum of Fine Arts has always been a museum ahead of its time. In addition to the AMFA Foundation Collection, the Museum established an art school and a children's theatre program in the 1960s and 1970s, both of which are still thriving. Progressive for those decades, this combination of visual and performing arts remains one of the trademarks of the institution.

AMFA's newest gateway to the future is manifest in its reimagined building and expanded grounds. The design concept is notably different from the 20th-century museum model of a grand entrance, box-shaped galleries, and a lecture hall for programs, for example, all of which served to define a building as a "museum." As necessity and demand required, eventually this model expanded and retail spaces and restaurants were added to enhance the visitor experience. That design, however, proves inadequate today, as museums aim to serve ever-expansive audiences whose interests and expectations require more from their visits.

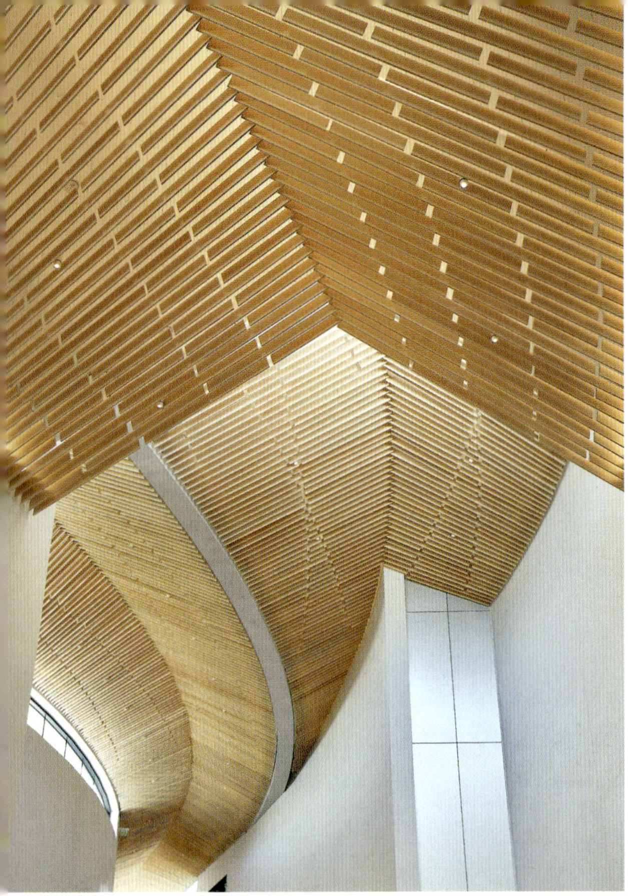

The repeating pattern of the slatted-wood ceiling and the light streaming through the Atrium's clerestory windows inspire feelings of awe.

The reimagined AMFA is a 21st-century museum. The building and grounds have been designed to be welcoming as well as intellectually and physically accessible. Social areas have been added for gathering. The resulting campus is a flexible space that will adapt and respond to the needs of the Museum and the surrounding community as they evolve. The building reflects what AMFA is, and will be, as an institution.

The building and the incredible views it affords are truly awe-inspiring, yet the Museum is comfortable, never overwhelming. The soaring height and carefully selected architectural details of the central Atrium signal that this is an exceptional place—one ready to support and inspire the community. As visitors enter the Museum and gaze up at the breathtaking ceiling, with its thousands of suspended wooden slats, we hope they realize: "This museum is a special space, one designed just for me."

The future of the arts, and of museums, is yet to be determined, but flexible programming spaces will allow AMFA to adapt as the world changes. For today's visual artists, dancers, and performers who create work in unconventional spaces, the Cultural Living Room, the Museum's signature gathering space, will be a nexus where artists and community connect. The Atrium can evolve into a gallery, with hang points on the ceiling offering visitors the chance to see art from a new angle. The Glass Box, a former back-of-house area, has been transformed into a light-filled space with an adjoining terrace and access to the outdoors.

How we define a 21st-century museum will undoubtedly evolve. For AMFA's next chapter, we are poised for the future.

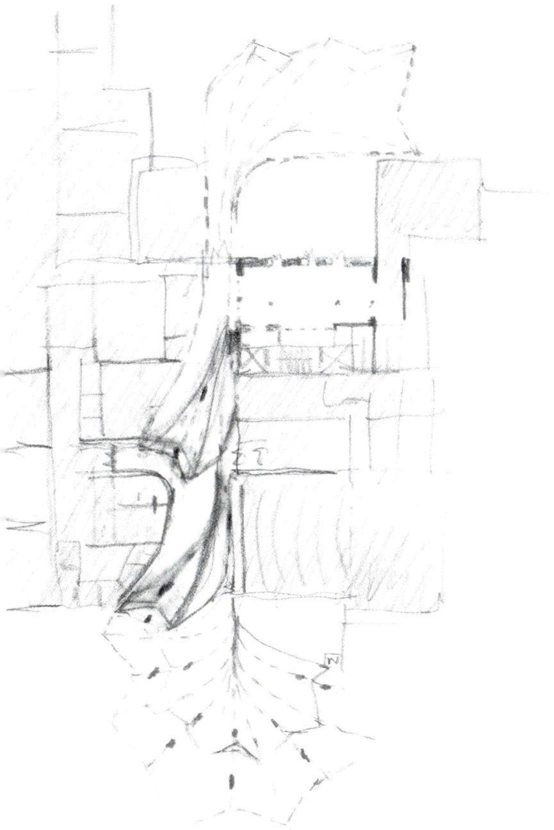

An early sketch by Jeanne Gang, exploring how the central stem can tie into the Museum's existing structure and foundations to bring AMFA's eight different buildings into a harmonious whole.

Jeanne Gang (Belvidere, Illinois, 1964 –), *Untitled Sketch*, 2017, graphite on vellum, 11 x 8 ½ in.

Reflections: Breathing New Life into a Beloved Community Connector

Jeanne Gang, Founding Principal and Partner, Studio Gang

From our first day on the AMFA project, we were struck by the Museum's rare strength as a community connector. With its Art School, Children's Theatre, and galleries, the Museum was home to a diverse program that appealed to many different people, and it had become a well-loved part of life in Little Rock. AMFA had already accomplished what so many museums are trying to do today: build community.

We heard from the AMFA team that they wanted to strengthen this special quality even further—to welcome and connect even more people with the arts—while also elevating the overall experience of the Museum and improving its functionality. Learning more about the existing AMFA facilities, we began to envision how this tight cluster of inward-facing structures could be reorganized and liberated to embrace—and be embraced by—both the community and the surrounding ecology of MacArthur Park.

I often use the phrase "start with what's there" to describe our Studio's design approach, meaning that we build on the existing positive qualities of a place to unfold new possibilities. This is exactly what we did to transform AMFA. First, we wanted to celebrate the variety of Museum programs that were already established and loved by the community. We also wanted to renew and reuse as much of the old building as possible, especially its structure and foundations, as a sustainable approach. At the

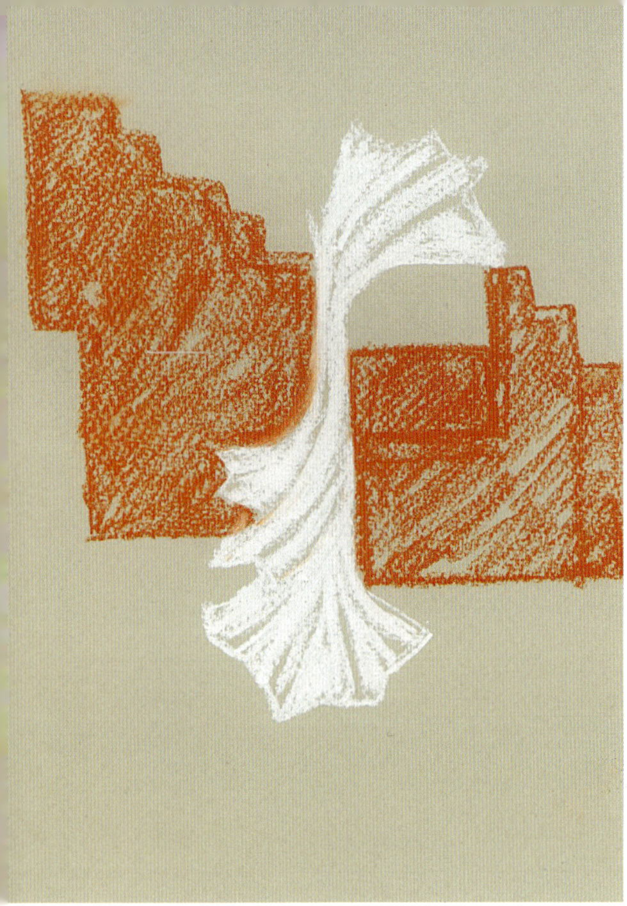

An early sketch by Jeanne Gang shows how the new central stem reorganizes the existing AMFA building, depicted in rust color, and "blossoms" into new spaces at the north and south.

Jeanne Gang (Belvidere, Illinois, 1964 –), *Untitled Sketch*, 2017, chalk on watercolor paper, 12 x 9 in.

same time, we wanted to help reposition AMFA with state-of-the-art facilities and an architecture that would energize visitors' experience of the Museum and give it a fresh identity.

To accomplish these goals, our design reorganized the flow along a new, central spine emerging outward at the north and south to form distinctive entrances and new public spaces. Like a blossom unfurling, this central form grows organically from the existing building and extends into the park and renewed landscape—breathing new life into the Museum and beckoning people to come together.

Inside, this organizing concept extends to the new and rejuvenated spaces that branch off from the central spine. Considering each space on its own and as part of the larger whole, we made strategic improvements to reinforce their function and character, while weaving them together through shared views and physical connections. You can see where you want to go and always feel connected to the outdoors with the abundance of natural light and views out to the park.

I'm delighted that the transformed AMFA campus is now taking on a life of its own. I hope everyone who visits this place senses the care and creative energy that went into its making, and feels invited and excited to become part of its vibrant community.

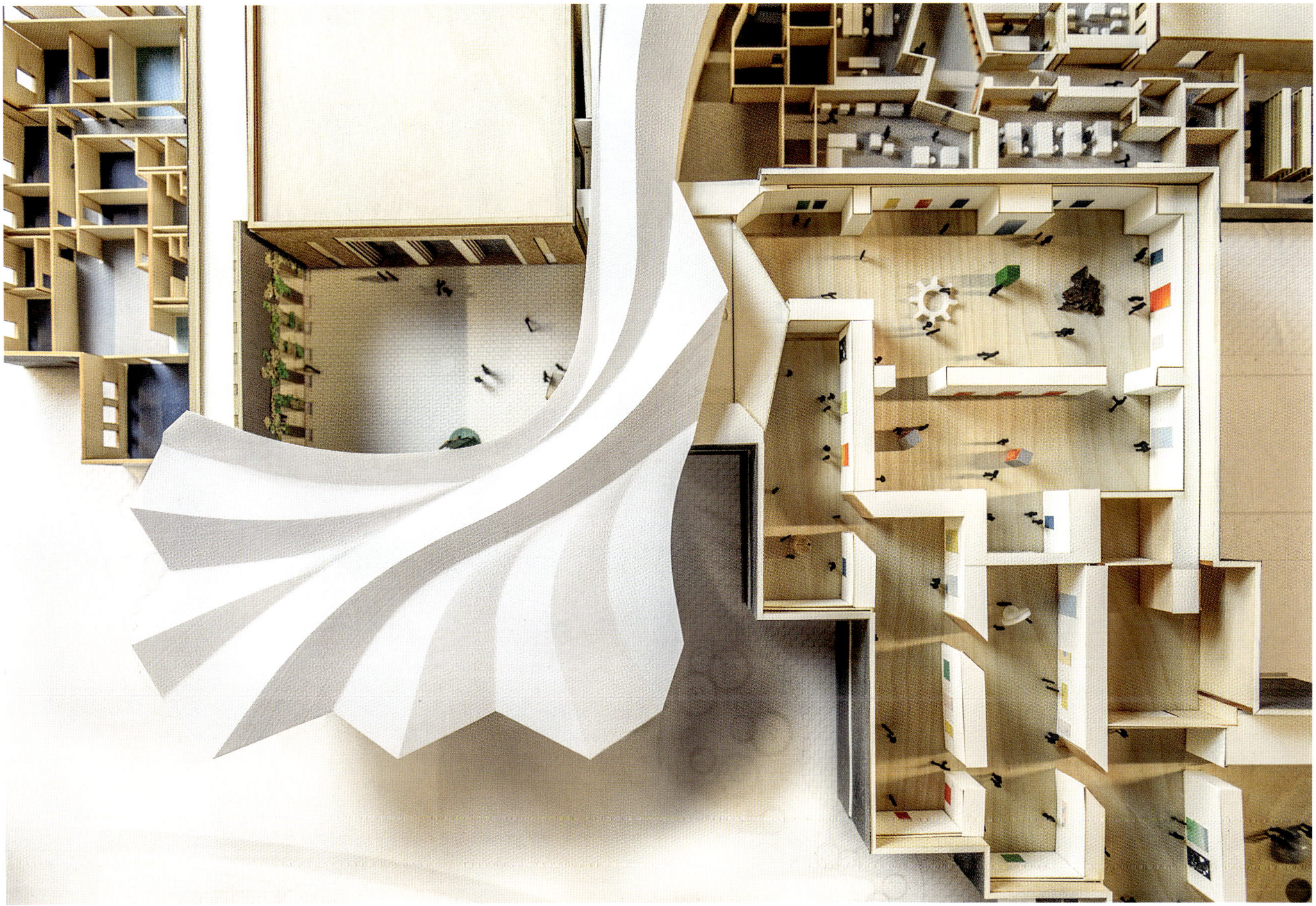

As shown in this scale model of the building, the organic form of the new roof expresses the vibrant, vital quality of AMFA's programming and role in the community.

Studio Gang (founded 1997, Chicago, Illinois), *Arkansas Museum of Fine Arts Scale Model*, 2019, museum board, wood, acrylic, paper, 10 x 50 x 66 in., scale: ⅛″ = 1′0″

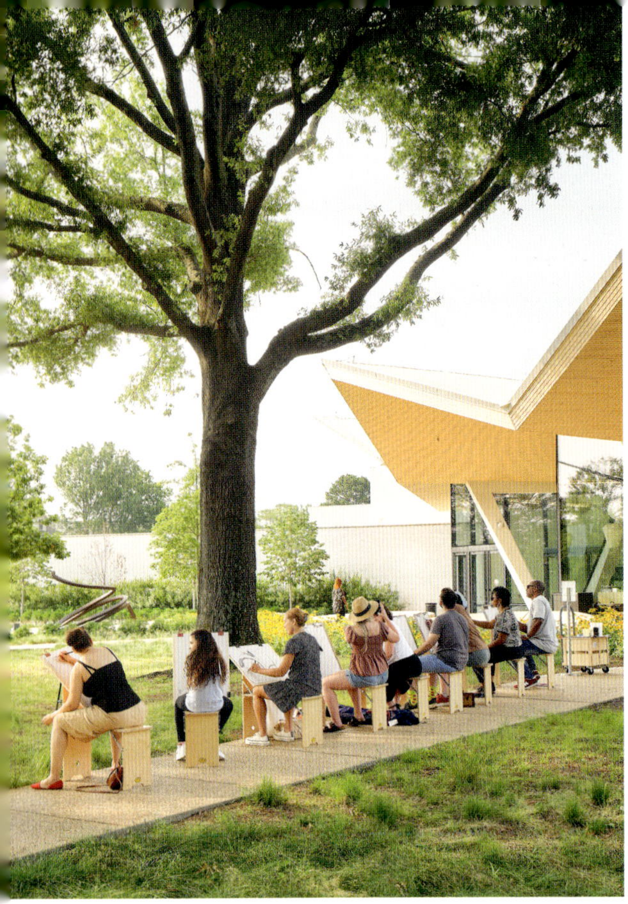

The new design incorporates opportunities for art appreciation across the grounds, with an expanded open-air sculpture collection, art production space, and flexible lawns for public events and performances.

Living Landscapes as Cultural Expression

Kate Orff, Founding Principal and Partner, SCAPE

Landscapes aren't static spaces. They are composed of living, growing organisms. Too often, museum grounds are purely formal expressions designed as backdrops that please the modern eye while suppressing life within. At AMFA, we worked to create a framework that provides not only an elegant setting for an incredible collection of art and sculpture, but also a robust biological matrix for life to thrive at all scales—bees hibernating in spent perennial stems, salamanders cooling under the rocks, migrating warblers darting around the oak canopy.

The Museum's central architectural gesture flows through and beyond the building from north to south, visually and physically merging the museum with its surroundings. The folded-plate roof serves a dual purpose, welcoming visitors while channeling rainwater to the surrounding terrain. At the Park Entrance, petal-shaped stormwater gardens capture and filter water from eaves in the roof, feathering out into the park and framing views beyond. At the Courtyard Entrance, subtly arcing pathways run alongside Crescent Drive toward downtown Little Rock, bordered by native meadow grasses and a diverse understory that supports native caterpillars, butterflies, and birds.

Surrounding the Museum is a mix of more than 250 new oaks, the predominant tree in the MacArthur Park, Little Rock's oldest municipal park. In time, these young trees will mature and merge with the existing canopy. Oaks are a legacy tree with

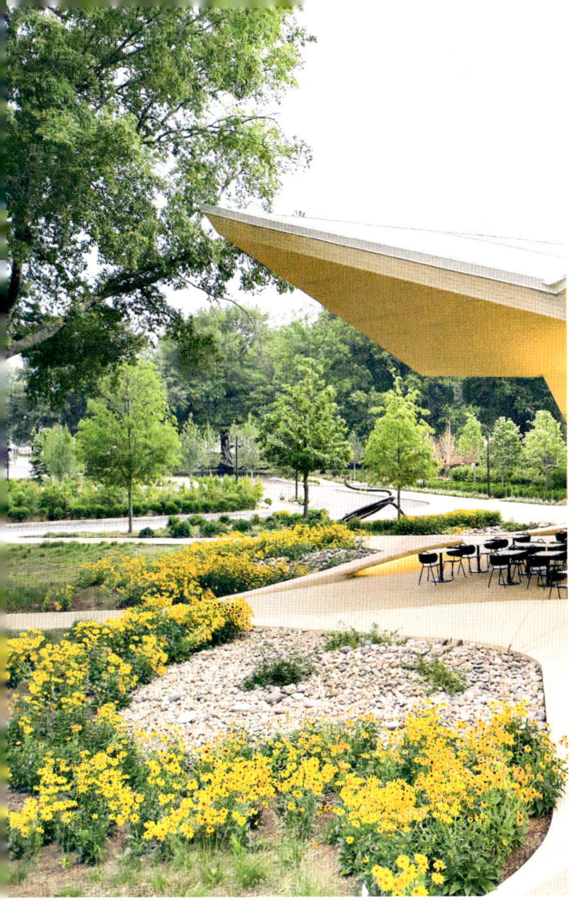

incredible ecological benefits, pumping carbon into the soil, providing shade on hot summer days, and forming the foundation of nature's food web. They also draw a crowd—more than 500 species of caterpillar feed on their leaves. Later, these pupae will molt into butterflies and moths that pollinate the Museum's gardens. Nesting songbirds will nourish their young with caterpillars, and those birds, once older, will feed on the fragrant berries of the wax myrtles planted in the surrounding gardens, distributing their seeds.

In this web of relationships, each tier of life supports and depends on the next. While visitors enjoy the sculptures and paintings of exceptional artists within the walls of the Museum, they can also marvel at the beauty and precarity of the living planet that we are making, intentionally and not, just outside.

To the south, the landscape features a series of petal-shaped stormwater gardens that extend the museum's architectural language outdoors, each given form by precast seatwalls and "splash pads" that capture stormwater runoff from the building's iconic folded-plate roof.

Elegant seatwalls emerge from the garden and frame a spill-out plaza space with informal seating, native perennials, and views to MacArthur Park.

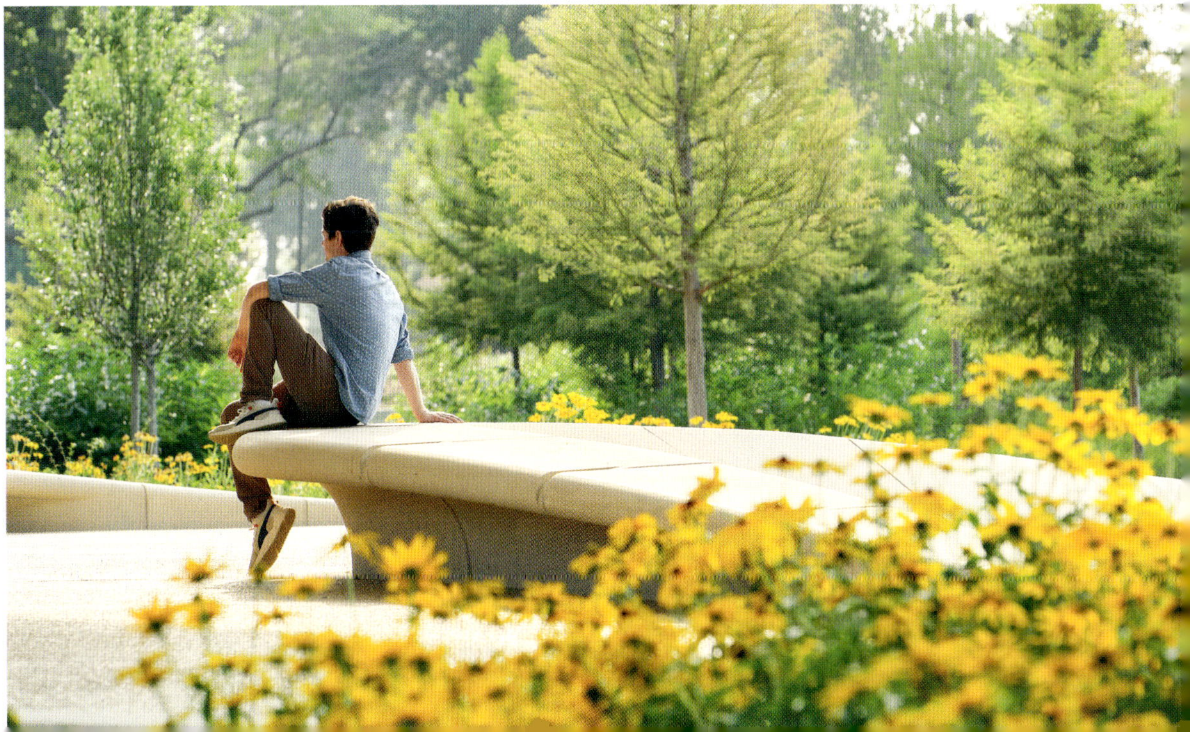

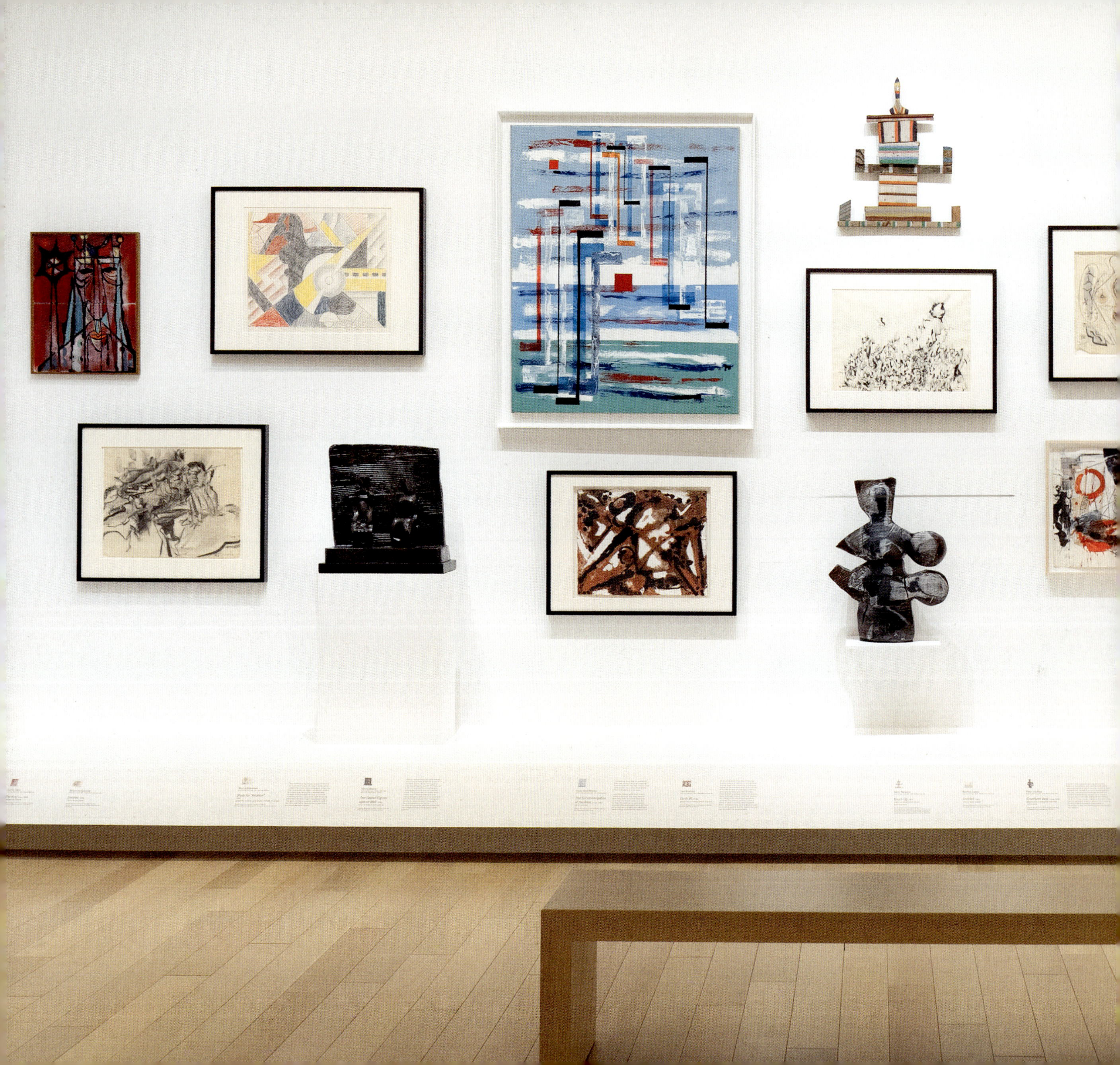

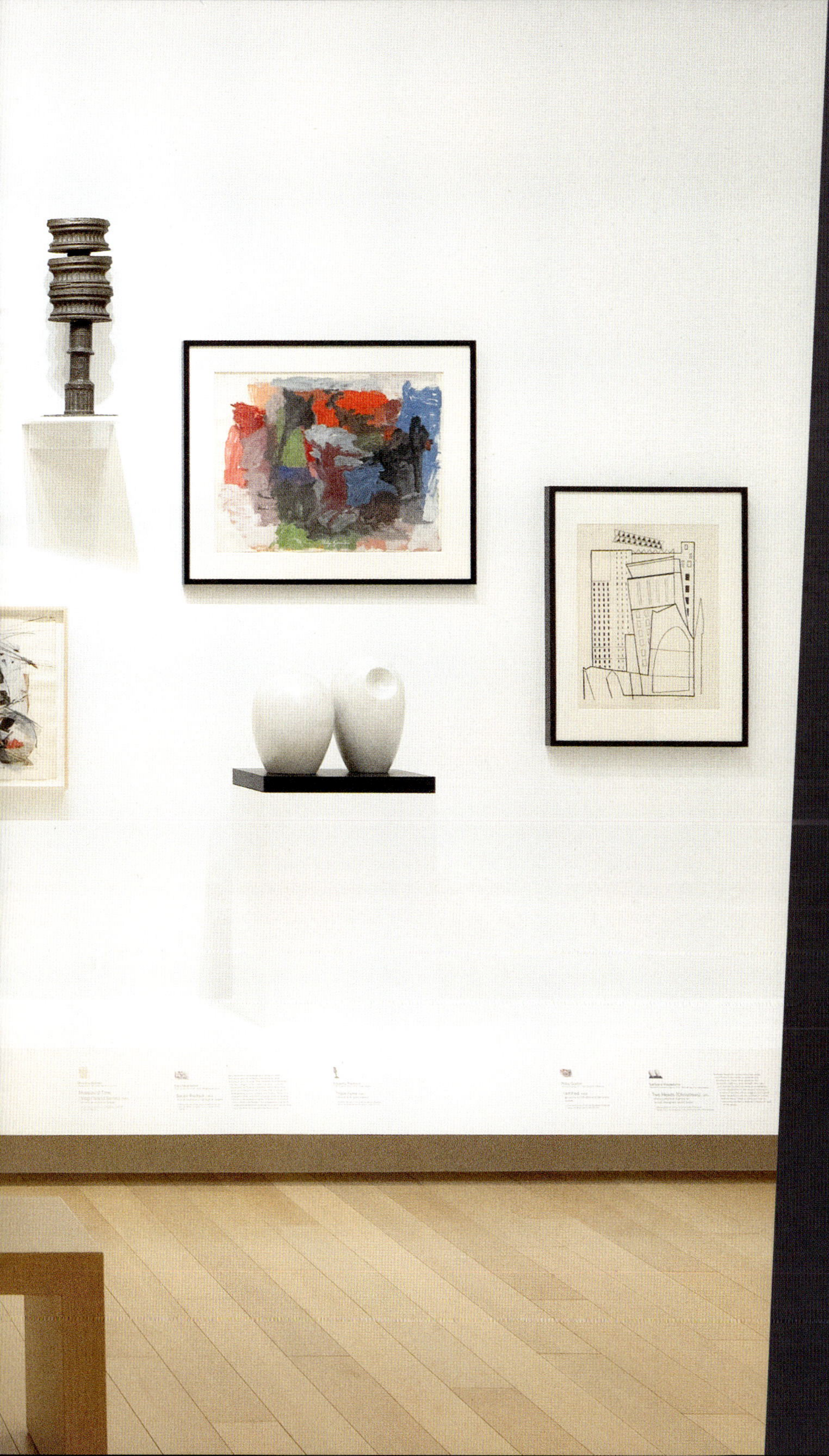

The AMFA Foundation Collection

The Arkansas Museum of Fine Arts Foundation Collection boasts more than 14,000 works and spans seven centuries, with strengths in works on paper and contemporary craft. Established in 1928 by members of Little Rock's Fine Arts Club, the collection now features artworks made in the Americas, Europe, Africa, and Asia. These selections highlight notable moments in the history of the AMFA Foundation Collection.

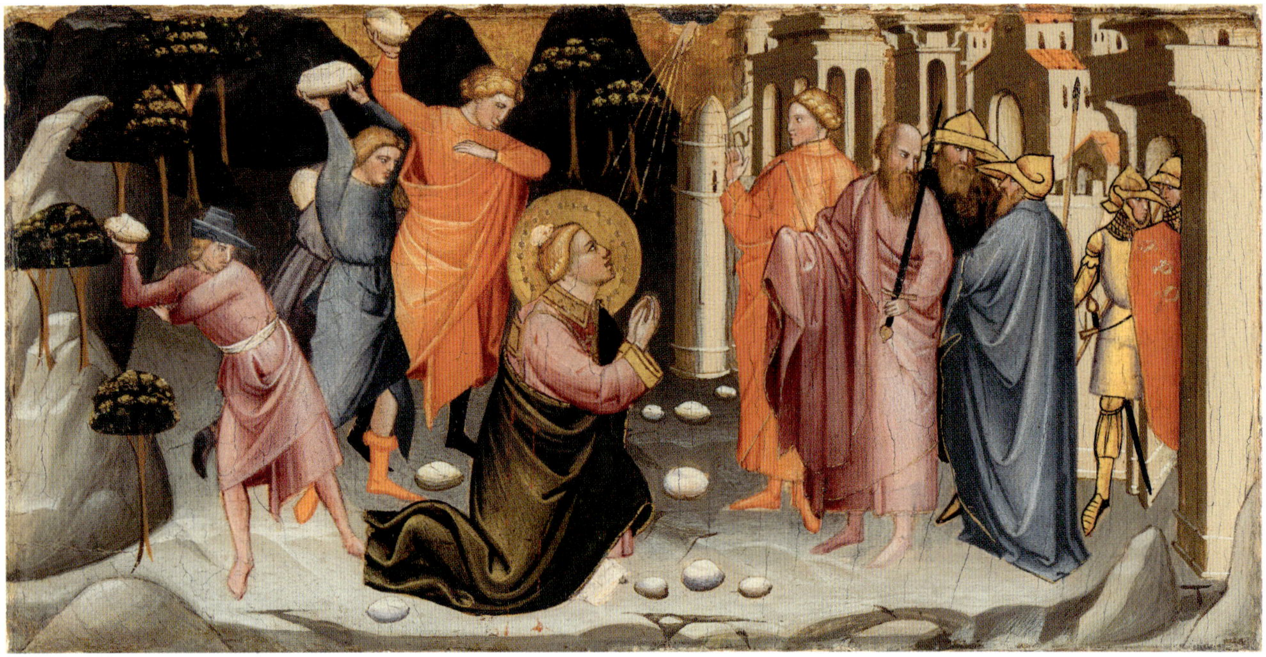

Attributed to **LORENZO DI NICCOLÒ**

In the 1930s, the Samuel H. Kress Foundation gave the fledging AMFA two Italian Renaissance paintings, including *Martyrdom of St. Stephen* (circa 1400), attributed to Lorenzo di Niccolò. The artist intended this painting, which was made for a large altarpiece, to communicate the story of St. Stephen to worshipers who never had the opportunity to learn to read, which was common for the time. Appointed by the Catholic Church to care for the elderly, widows, and orphans, St. Stephen became the first Christian martyr in 36 CE, after he was stoned to death outside the gates of Jerusalem. As the story's subject, the saint appears in the center of the composition, depicted slightly larger than the other figures. The halo encircling his head uses gold to symbolize his holiness as he kneels in prayer, asking God to forgive his murderers.

Attributed to **Lorenzo di Niccolò** (Active in Florence, Italy, 1391 – 1412), *Martyrdom of St. Stephen*, circa 1400, tempera and gold on wood panel, 9 ½ x 19 ⅛ x 2 in., Arkansas Museum of Fine Arts Foundation Collection: Gift of the Samuel H. Kress Foundation. 1939.002.

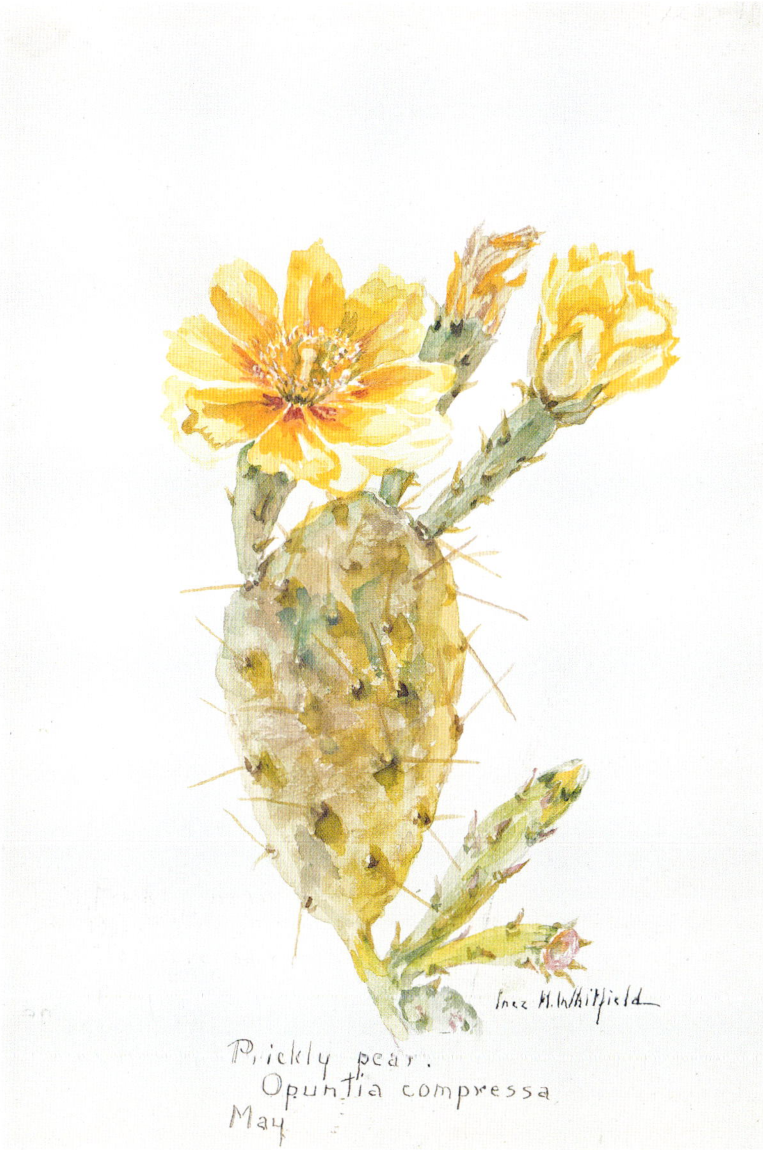

INEZ WHITFIELD

In the first half of the 20th century, Inez Whitfield created more than 500 paintings of Arkansas flora with a conservationist's attention to detail. A native of New York State, Whitfield relocated to Hot Springs, Arkansas, to take mineral baths for her rheumatoid arthritis. On good days, she hiked the wooded hills that would become Hot Springs National Park, searching for specimens to document. By 1911, she used a wheelchair, but friends brought wildflowers to her studio, replanting them after she finished her paintings. Whitfield's work gained wide admiration for its educational value and its testament to Arkansas's natural beauty. To help cover the artist's medical bills, garden clubs and women's groups across the state raised $5,000—$83,000 in today's money—to purchase 367 of her works for the AMFA Foundation Collection in 1945. More than a century after Whitfield picked up a paintbrush, her life's work remains a time capsule of Arkansas's environment in a rapidly changing climate.

Inez Whitfield (German Flatts, New York, 1867 – 1951, Hot Springs, Arkansas), *Prickly pear: Opuntia compressa (May)*, circa 1935, watercolor on paper, 10 x 7 in., Arkansas Museum of Fine Arts Foundation Collection: Gift of the Arkansas Federation of Garden Clubs. 1945.009.249.

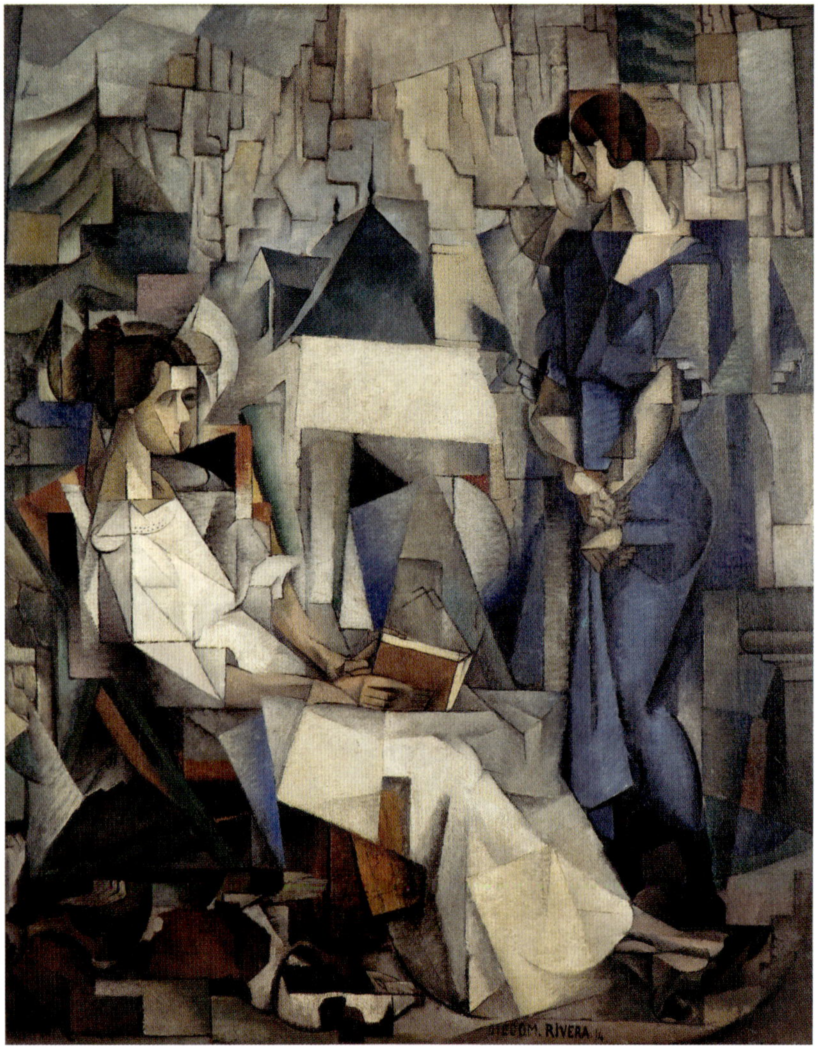

DIEGO RIVERA

Although he is best known for his large-scale fresco murals in public settings, Mexican artist Diego Rivera lived in Europe from 1907 to 1921, soaking up the influences of Cubism and painting in oil on canvas. The fractured interlacing of a cozy interior scene and an exterior view of Paris in *Dos Mujeres (Two Women)* demonstrates Cubism's impact—multiple rectangular shapes and angles reveal both tableaus. Rivera's common-law wife, Russian artist Angelina Beloff, posed for the work, facing her friend Russian-Cuban painter Alma Dolores Bastián, who sits in the chair next to a sleeping dog.

Abby Rockefeller Mauzé, sister of future Arkansas Governor Winthrop Rockefeller, donated *Dos Mujeres* to AMFA in 1955. Along with his wife, Jeanette, Rockefeller launched a fundraising campaign in 1959 to create a statewide center for the arts. In 1960, the Little Rock Board of Directors adopted an ordinance officially establishing the Arkansas Arts Center, and the new building—an addition to the 1937 museum—opened in 1963.

Diego Rivera (Guanajuato, Mexico, 1886 – 1957, Mexico City, Mexico), *Dos Mujeres (Two Women)*, 1914, oil on canvas, 77 ¾ x 63 ½ in., Arkansas Museum of Fine Arts Foundation Collection: Gift of Abby Rockefeller Mauzé. 1955.010. © 2023 Banco de México Diego Rivera Frida Kahlo Museums Trust, Mexico, D.F. / Artists Rights Society (ARS), New York.

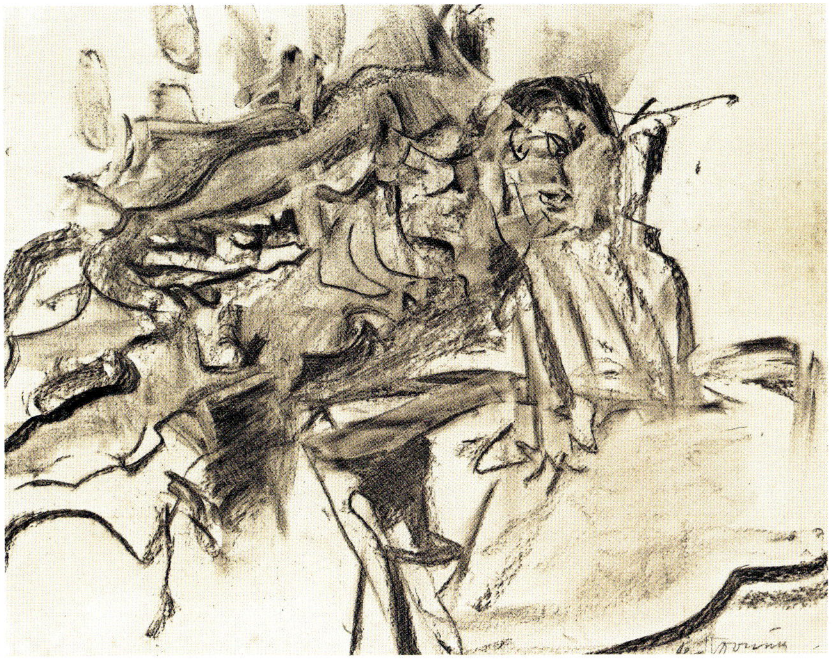

WILLEM DE KOONING

AMFA used funds from its first National Endowment for the Arts Museum Purchase Grant to acquire three drawings in 1971, including this untitled 1969 work by Willem de Kooning. This purchase marked the beginning of the Museum's dedication to collecting drawings.

In the late 1940s and early 1950s, de Kooning and his contemporaries working in New York City gained attention for their emotive abstract paintings. De Kooning's most famous works were his *Women* paintings, which used aggressive brushstrokes to depict archetypes of women rather than detailed portraits. The female figure remained an important subject throughout the artist's career, as evidenced by this drawing he created after moving out of the city to a studio on Long Island. This drawing fragments elements of the figure—a face, arms, torso, feet—which dissolve into the surrounding turbulent lines.

Willem de Kooning (Rotterdam, Holland, 1904 – 1997, East Hampton, New York), *Untitled*, 1969, charcoal on paper, 19 x 24 in., Arkansas Museum of Fine Arts Foundation Collection: Purchase, Tabriz Fund and Museum Purchase Plan of the NEA. 1971.009.002.

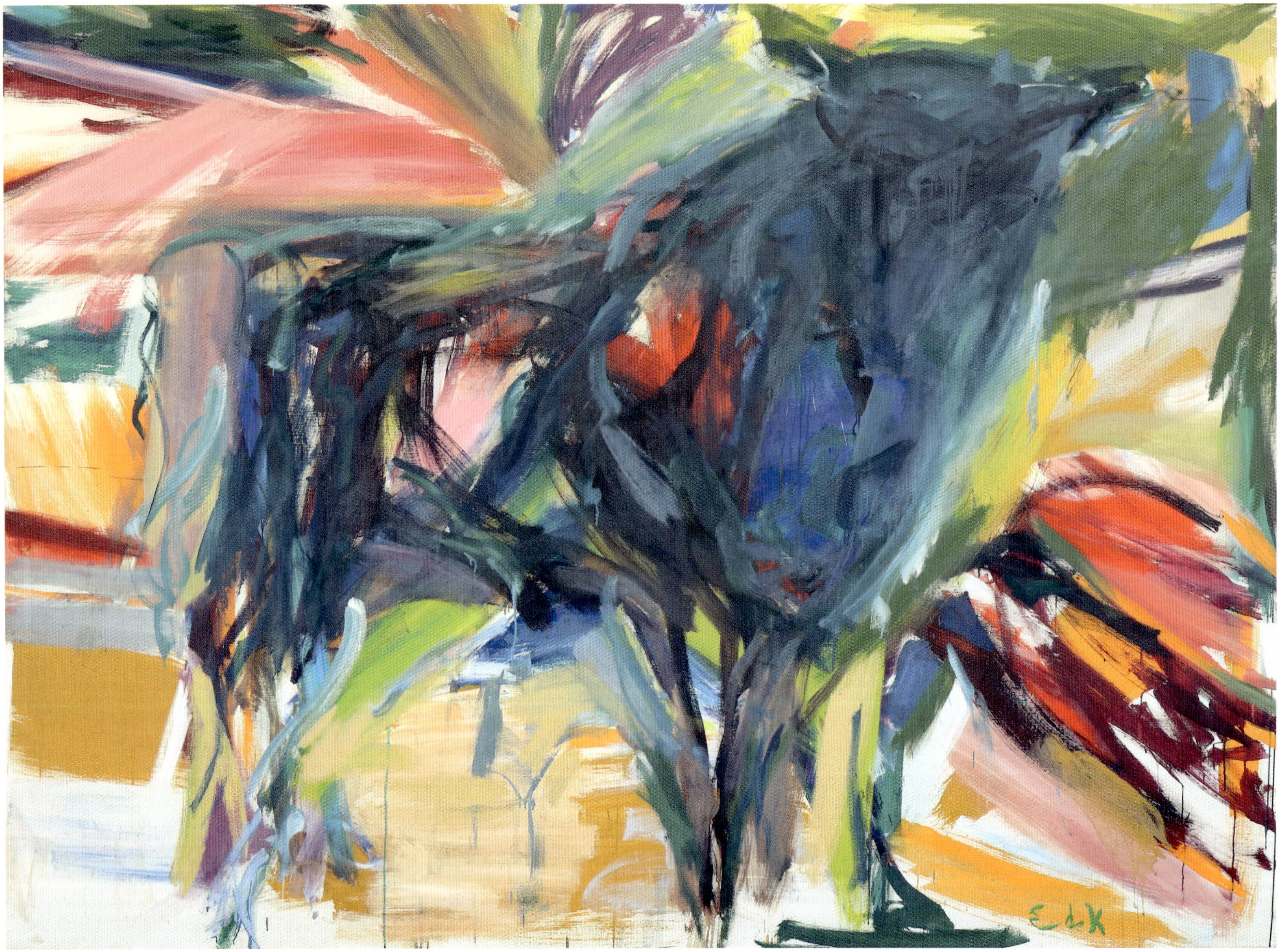

ELAINE DE KOONING

In December 1972, Elaine de Kooning taught a three-day portrait painting master class at AMFA's Windgate Art School. Around the same time, a friend of de Kooning's, sculptor Robert Mallary, offered AMFA *Standing Bull* (1958) as a donation. Mallary helped de Kooning, who was then separated from her husband, Willem, obtain a visiting professorship at the University of New Mexico in the late 1950s. The two made frequent weekend trips to Juarez, Mexico. There, de Kooning took in the sights, sounds, and smells of bullfights, making quick pastel drawings of the rushing animals. Back in her studio, she referred to those studies to make large-scale paintings, such as *Standing Bull*, that express the explosive power and energy of the bulls through brilliant colors and frenetic brushstrokes.

Elaine de Kooning (New York, New York, 1918 – 1989, Southampton, New York), *Standing Bull*, 1958, oil and acrylic on canvas, 78 ¼ x 108 ¼ in., Arkansas Museum of Fine Arts Foundation Collection: Gift of Robert Mallary. 1973.024.

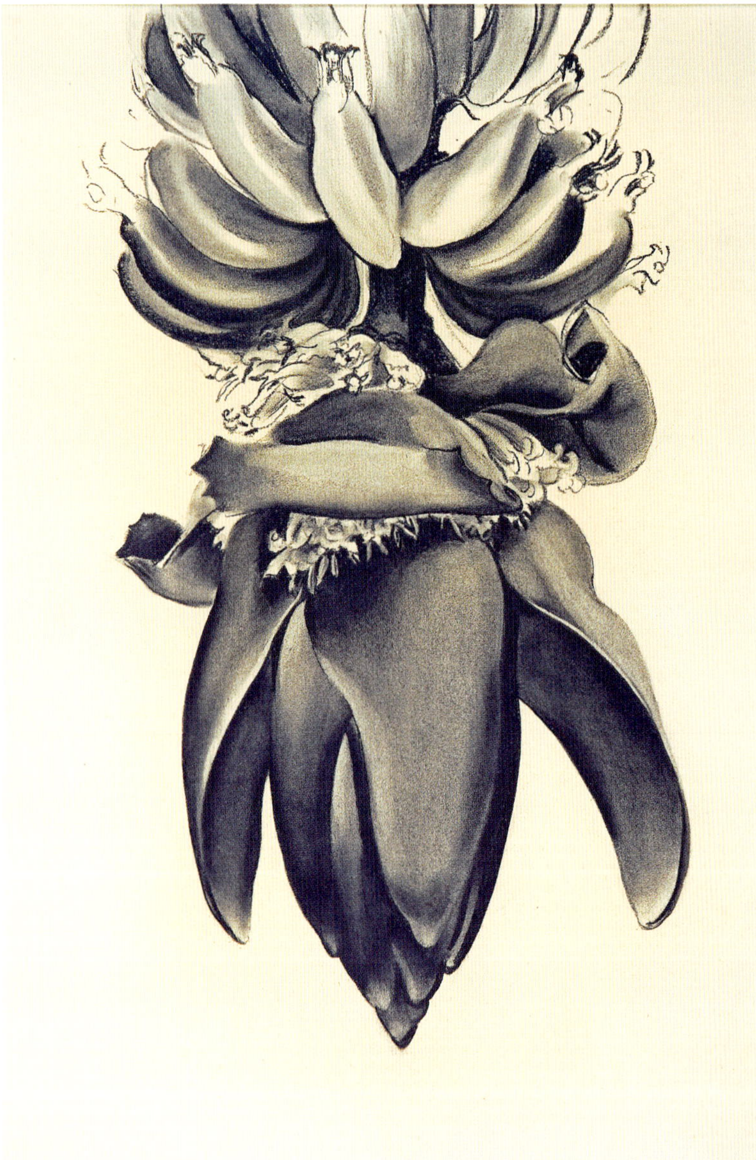

GEORGIA O'KEEFFE

In 1974 AMFA purchased its first work by Georgia O'Keeffe, *Special No. 30 (Banana Flower)* (1934), one of a series of five drawings depicting blossoms. O'Keeffe made this work while visiting Bermuda to recover from a bout of depression, sketching the bloom of a banana plant growing on the grounds of the villa where she stayed. While she is better known as a painter, charcoal drawing played an important role in her career. In 1915, a friend secretly showed O'Keeffe's abstract charcoal drawings to influential gallerist Alfred Stieglitz, leading to her first New York gallery showing. Today, O'Keeffe's distinctive style and personal story make her a feminist art icon.

Georgia O'Keeffe (Sun Prairie, Wisconsin, 1887–1986, Santa Fe, New Mexico), *Special No. 30 (Banana Flower)*, 1934, charcoal on paper, 22 x 15 in., Arkansas Museum of Fine Arts Foundation Collection: Purchase, Tabriz Fund and Museum Purchase Plan of the NEA. 1974.011.008. © 2023 Georgia O'Keeffe Museum / Artists Rights Society (ARS), New York.

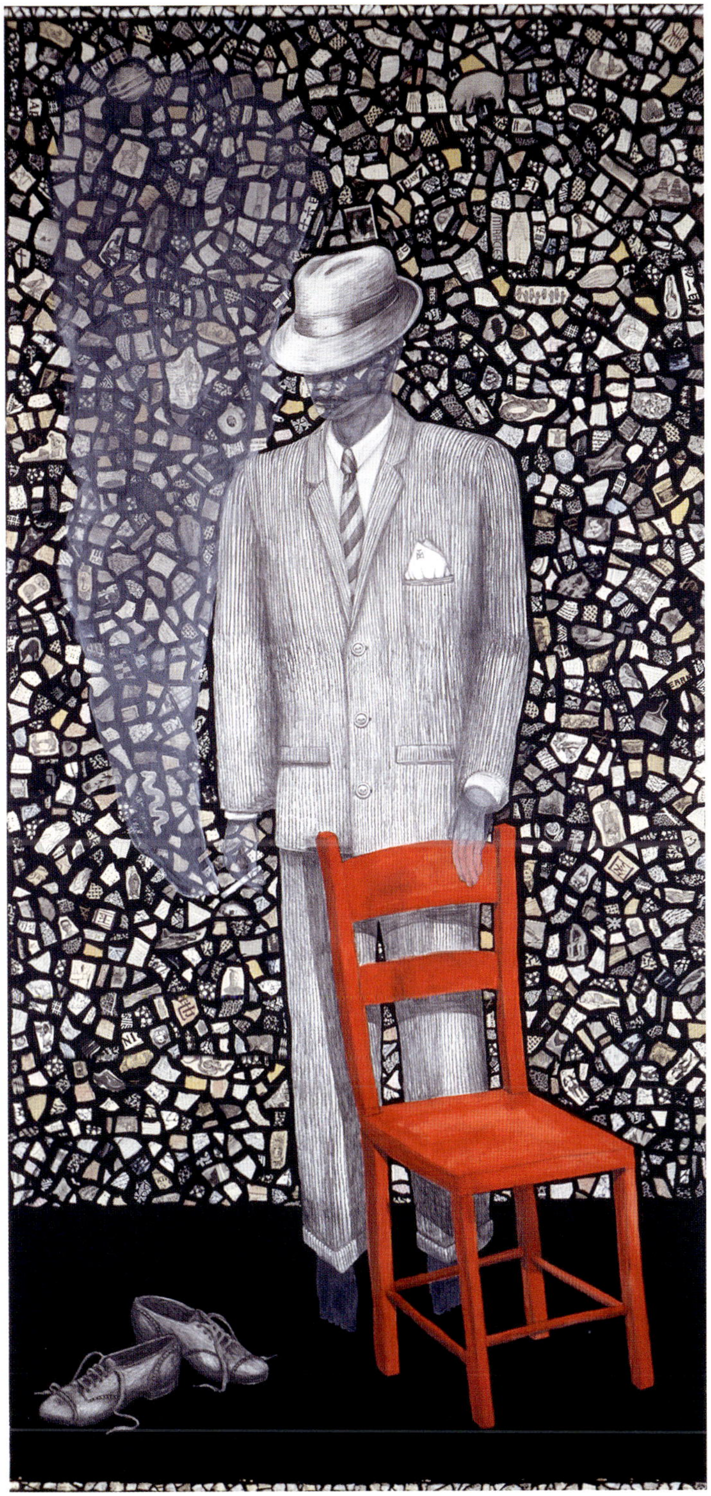

ALISON SAAR

Alison Saar taught a one-day workshop on drawing and collage in the AMFA's Windgate Art School and served as juror for the Delta Exhibition in May 2001. Begun in 1958, the Delta is a juried show open to submissions from Arkansas and its six surrounding states. AMFA has acquired many works by Delta Exhibition and Art School workshop artists; this one was purchased with funds from the National Endowment for the Arts and the Collectors Group. This collage of torn black-and-white images of abstract patterns, animals, and people of all races and genders forms the background of Saar's *Invisible Man* (1985). In the foreground, a faint figure dissipates, leaving behind his suit, cigarette, and chair. Saar's work shares the same title as Ralph Ellison's 1947 novel, which tells a story of a young Black man struggling to be seen as an authentic person rather than a stereotype.

Alison Saar (Los Angeles, California, 1956 –), *Invisible Man*, 1985, mixed media on paper, 104 x 50 in., Arkansas Museum of Fine Arts Foundation Collection: Purchase, Collectors Group Fund and Museum Purchase Plan of the NEA. 1990.023. © Alison Saar. Courtesy of L. A. Louver, Venice, CA.

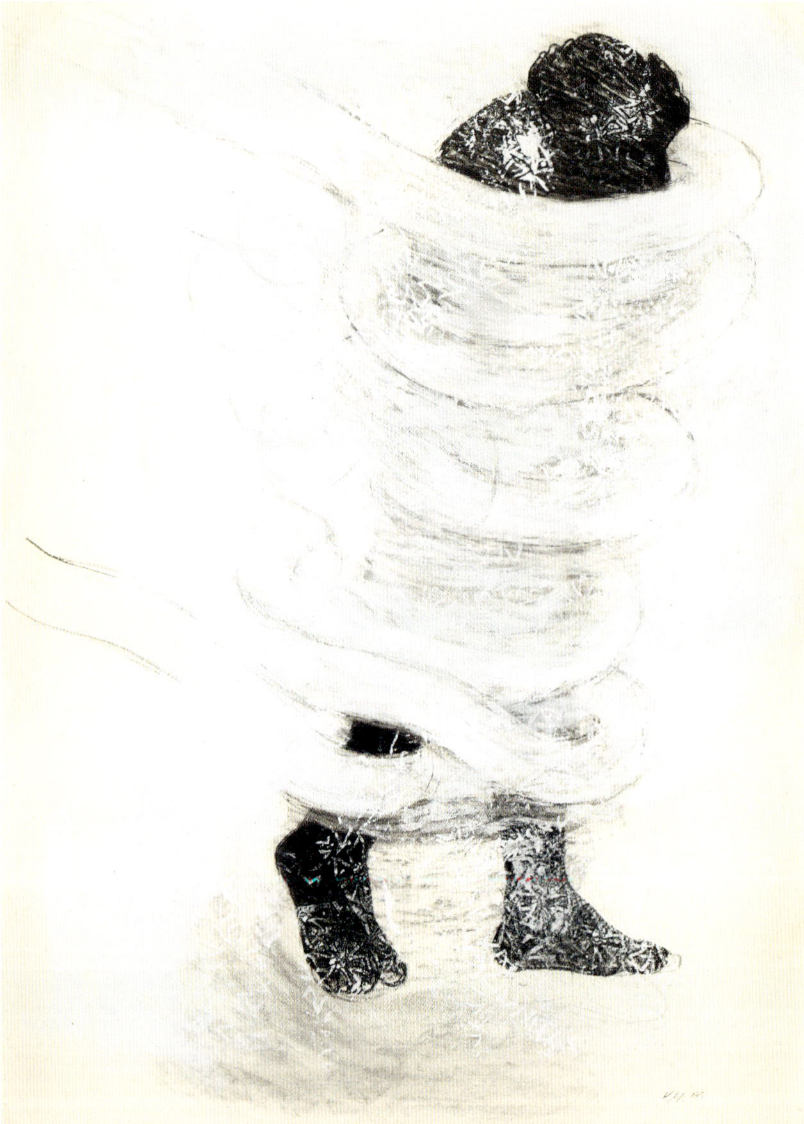

KERRY JAMES MARSHALL

AMFA hosted 12 National Drawing Invitationals between 1986 and 2014, acquiring works by artists selected for the exhibitions. Kerry James Marshall's *Cool Wind* (1985) appeared in the fourth Invitational, in 1992. Growing up in Los Angeles, Marshall noticed that paintings in art history books never featured Black people. He decided to dedicate his career to depicting African American subjects, rendering their bodies using rich black hues. "The lighter the skin, the more acceptable you are. The darker the skin, the more marginalized you become," Marshall notes. "I want to demonstrate that you can produce beauty in the context of a figure that has that kind of velvety blackness." The figure in *Cool Wind* appears as a flatly rendered silhouette, but in later works the artist has added more dimensionality to his subjects.

Kerry James Marshall (Birmingham, Alabama, 1956 –), *Cool Wind*, 1985, charcoal and acrylic on paper, 50 x 38 in., Arkansas Museum of Fine Arts Foundation Collection: Purchased with a bequest from Louise Long. 1991.023.003. © Kerry James Marshall. Courtesy of the artist and Jack Shainman Gallery, New York. Photography by Edward C. Robison III.

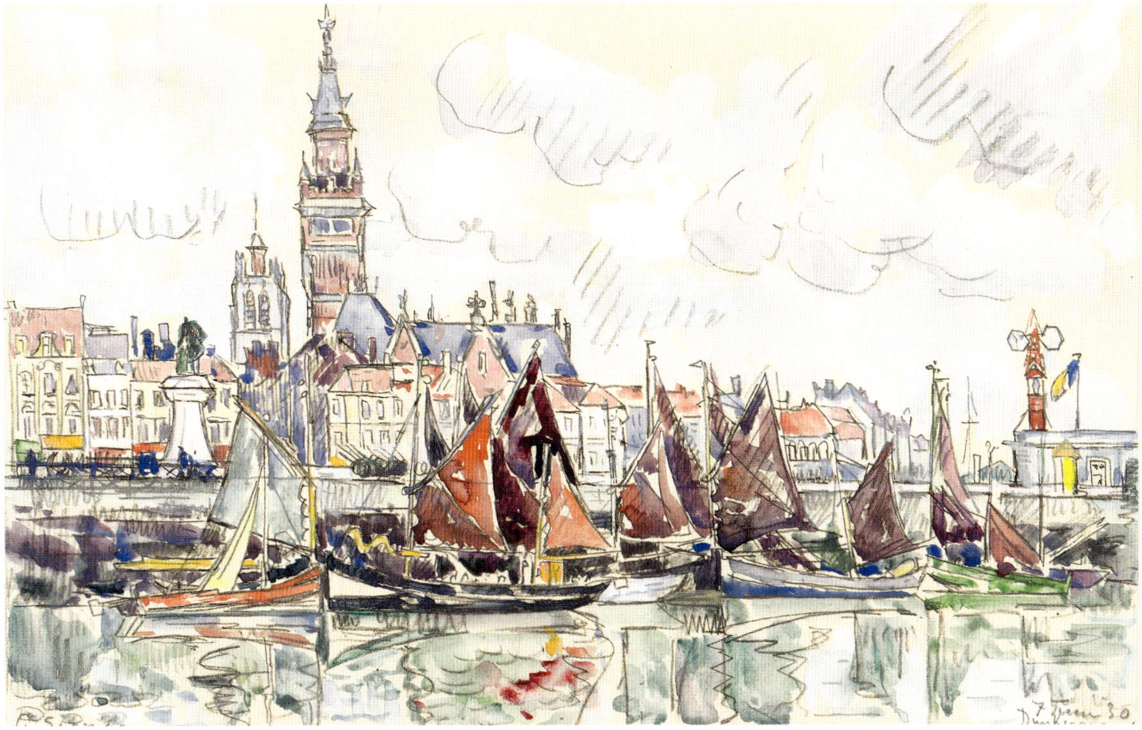

PAUL SIGNAC

AMFA is home to the largest collection of works by Paul Signac outside France. Arkansas lawyer and industrialist James T. Dyke donated 133 drawings and watercolors to the AMFA Foundation Collection in 1999 and 2000. A member of the Neo-Impressionists—artists who reproduced the effects of color and light using dots of pure color—Signac began experimenting with watercolors in 1892. By 1910, he had given up oil painting to focus exclusively on watercolor, and his technique evolved from dots to brushstrokes of pigment. Born into a wealthy family, Signac sailed yachts in France's rivers and canals and on the Mediterranean Sea, painting and drawing as he traveled. Businessman Gaston Lévy commissioned the artist to make watercolors of 100 French ports in 1929. The project kept Signac occupied until the summer of 1931—he completed a painting of each port for his patron and another to keep for himself. The "Ports of France" series makes up a portion of AMFA's holding of Signac watercolors, including this 1930 depiction of Dunkirk.

Paul Signac (Paris, France, 1863 – 1935, Paris, France), *Dunkerque (Dunkirk)*, 1930, watercolor and graphite on paper, 11 ¼ x 17 ¾ in., Arkansas Museum of Fine Arts Foundation Collection: Gift of James T. Dyke. 1999.065.098. Photography by Edward C. Robison III.

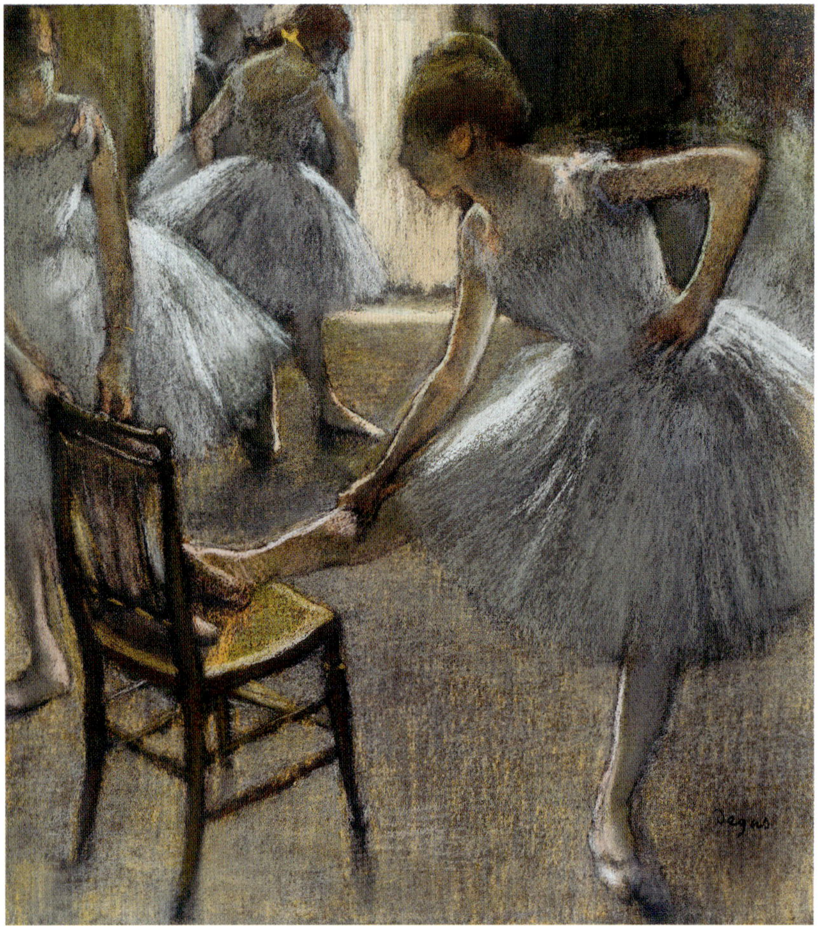

EDGAR HILAIRE GERMAIN DEGAS

The Jackson T. Stephens Charitable Trust for Art holds significant late 19th- and early 20th-century European and American works, long-term loans that AMFA has stewarded since 2000. The trust contains 23 total works, with 17 paintings and 6 works on paper.

This scene from the Stephens Trust work *Danseuse bleue (Blue Dancer)* (1886 – 1890) by Edgar Degas depicts the moment before a ballet class. The artist emphasized the dancers' feet and limbs as they stretch, particularly the raised calf of the foreground ballerina. Although Degas drew and painted the grace and glamour of onstage performances, the labor and boredom of the working class dancers behind the scenes equally captivated him, as demonstrated by this work.

Edgar Hilaire Germain Degas (Paris, France, 1834 – 1917, Paris, France), *Danseuse bleue (Avant la classe, trois danseuses), Blue Dancer (Before Class, Three Dancers)*, 1886 – 1890, pastel on paper, 21 ¼ x 19 ¾ in., On loan from the Jackson T. Stephens Charitable Trust for Art. Photography by Edward C. Robison III.

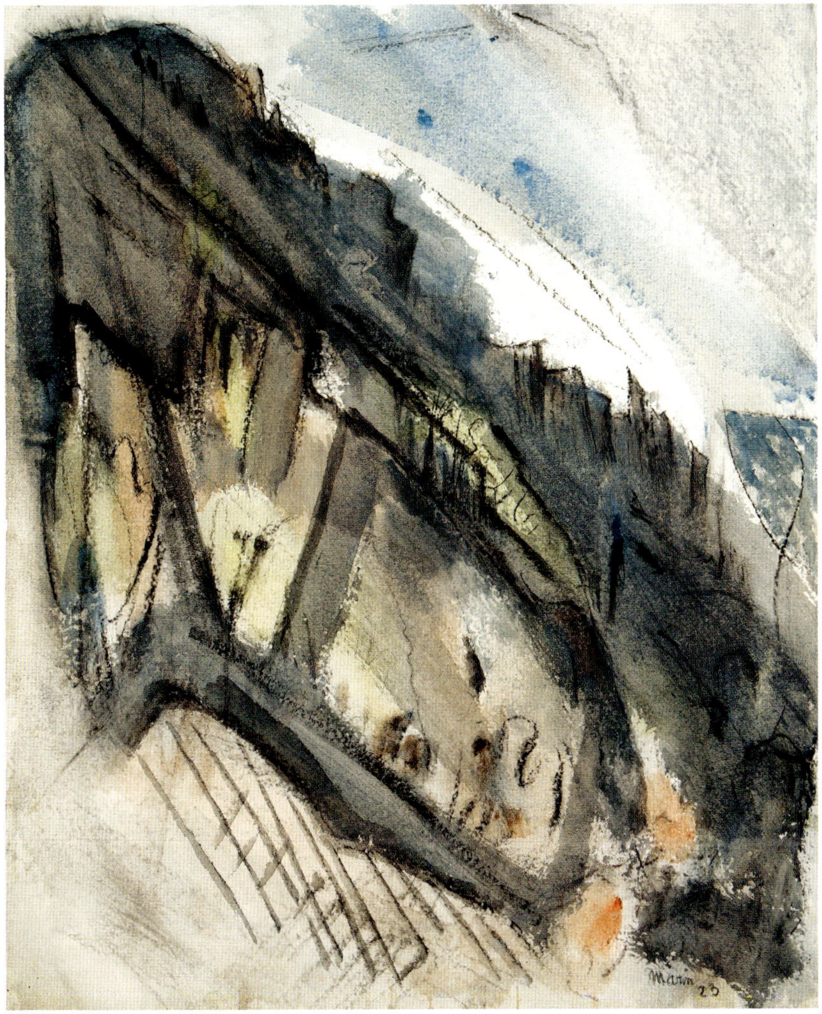

JOHN MARIN

John Marin earned critical acclaim in the early 20th century for his abstract landscapes painted in watercolors, exhibited at Alfred Stieglitz's gallery, 291. Marin's *Palisades* series is based on the rocky formations that connect New York and New Jersey. In *Palisades, Hudson River, New Jersey* (1923), Marin chose a steeply angled view that suggests gravity and speed. He outlined the rocks and abstract forms along the edge of the cliff in charcoal and painted earthy hues in loose, flowing washes of watercolor. The charcoal crosshatching at the bottom left of the composition adds to the sense of movement.

In 2013, Norma Marin donated 290 watercolors and drawings by her father-in-law, John Marin, to the AMFA Foundation Collection, making the museum the second-largest depository of work by the artist.

John Marin (Rutherford, New Jersey, 1870 – 1953, Cape Split, Maine), *Palisades, Hudson River, New Jersey*, 1923, watercolor and charcoal on textured watercolor paper, 19 ¾ x 16 ½ in., Arkansas Museum of Fine Arts Foundation Collection: Gift of Norma B. Marin. 2013.018.234. © 2023 Estate of John Marin / Artists Rights Society (ARS), New York. Courtesy Schoelkopf Gallery.

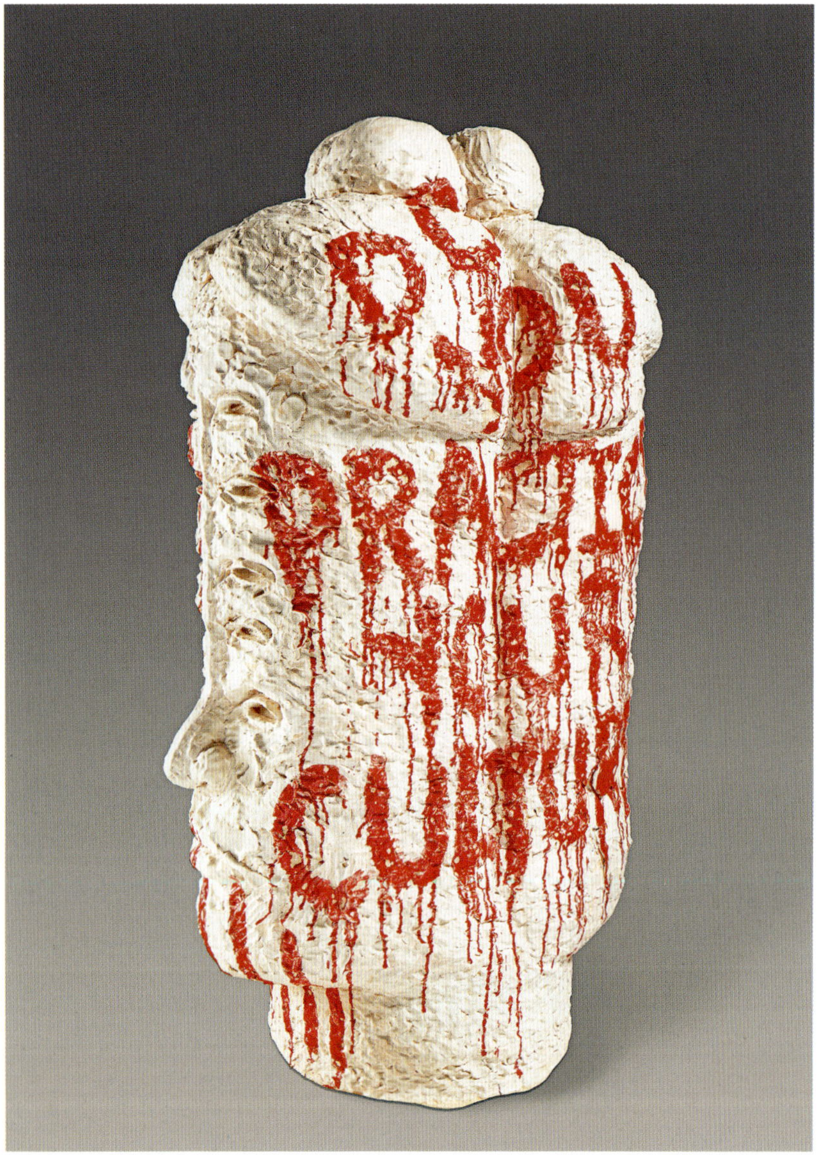

RAVEN HALFMOON

In October 2023, Raven Halfmoon became the second artist-in-residence in AMFA's Windgate Art School. Halfmoon, a member of the Caddo Nation, studied art and anthropology at the University of Arkansas, where she researched pottery made by her ancestors through the Arkansas Archaeological Survey. The artist's work melds her traditional tribal knowledge with her lived experience in the 21st century. The monumentally scaled form of *Do You Practice Your Culture?* (2019) consists of hand-built stacked and replicated totemic faces. Halfmoon scrawled the work's title in graffiti-like letters on one side and tagged her name on the other. "My name comes with a lot of history," she says. "It is a name that my great-great-grandfather lived with through boarding schools and genocide. It's a statement that we're still here."

Raven Halfmoon (Norman, Oklahoma, 1991 –), *Do You Practice Your Culture?*, 2019, glazed stoneware, 62 x 20 x 38 in., Arkansas Museum of Fine Arts Foundation Collection: Purchase. 2021.007.001. Photography by Edward C. Robison III.

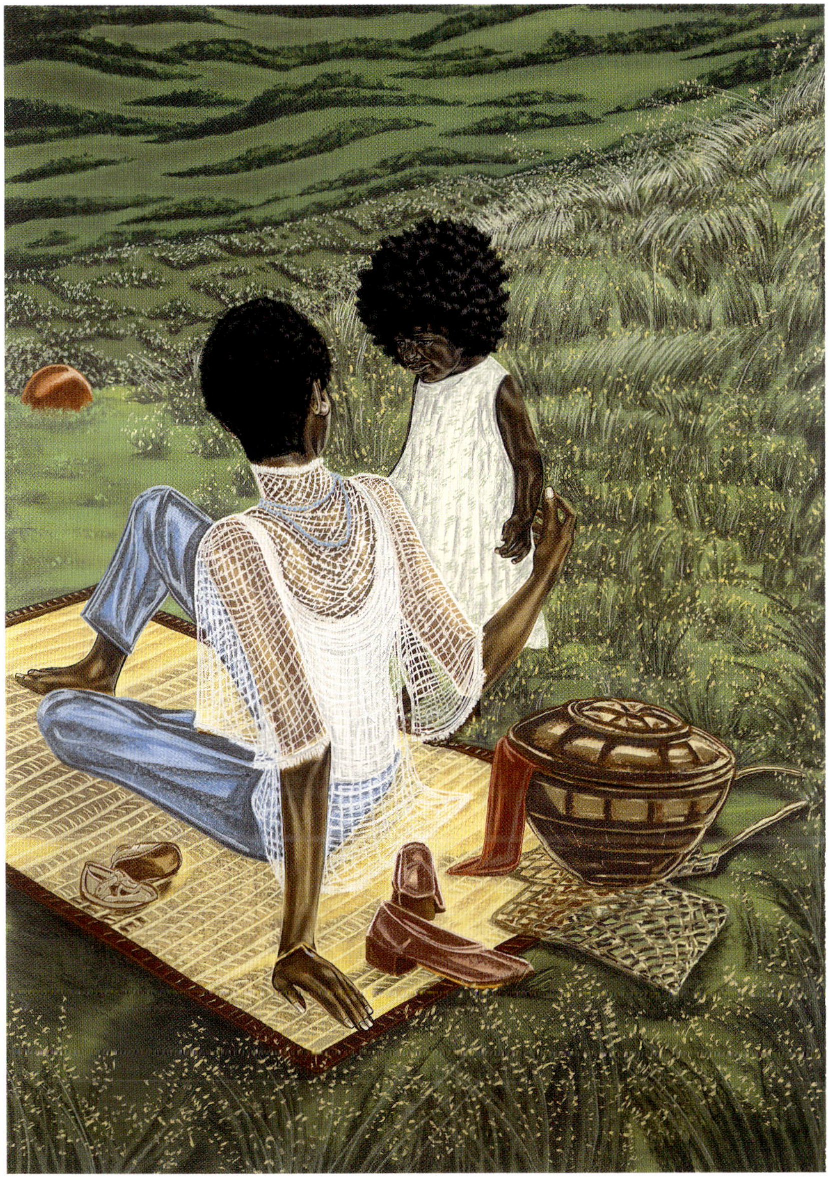

TOYIN OJIH ODUTOLA

Together, the inaugural exhibition in AMFA's Harriet and Warren Stephens Galleries, welcomed guests back to the Museum with art focused on connections among friends, family, community, and the natural world. *Together* debuted new acquisitions, including the pastel, charcoal, and pencil drawing *Picnic on the Grounds* by Toyin Ojih Odutola. Born in Nigeria and raised in Alabama, Ojih Odutola draws from her experience as an African American immigrant to question representations of Blackness in Western art history. This work depicts a mother and daughter lounging in a grassy field and calls to mind paintings of white Europeans at leisure by Impressionists such as Manet and Renoir. Ojih Odutola's mother and daughter, however, belong to the artist's series of portraits of two fictional aristocratic Nigerian families joined through marriage. Depicted in social interactions and at leisure in lush landscapes and opulent interiors, Ojih Odutola's fanciful family members present an alternative reality in which historically oppressed people thrive outside the legacies of global colonialism.

Toyin Ojih Odutola (Ilé-Ifẹ̀, Nigeria, 1985 –), *Picnic on the Grounds*, 2017 – 2018, pastel, charcoal, and graphite on paper, 69 ½ x 50 ¼ in., Arkansas Museum of Fine Arts Foundation Collection: Given in honor of the Grand Opening of the Reimagined Arkansas Museum of Fine Arts by Harriet and Warren Stephens, April 22, 2023. 2023.001. © Toyin Ojih Odutola. Courtesy of the artist and Jack Shainman Gallery, New York. Photography by Edward C. Robison III.

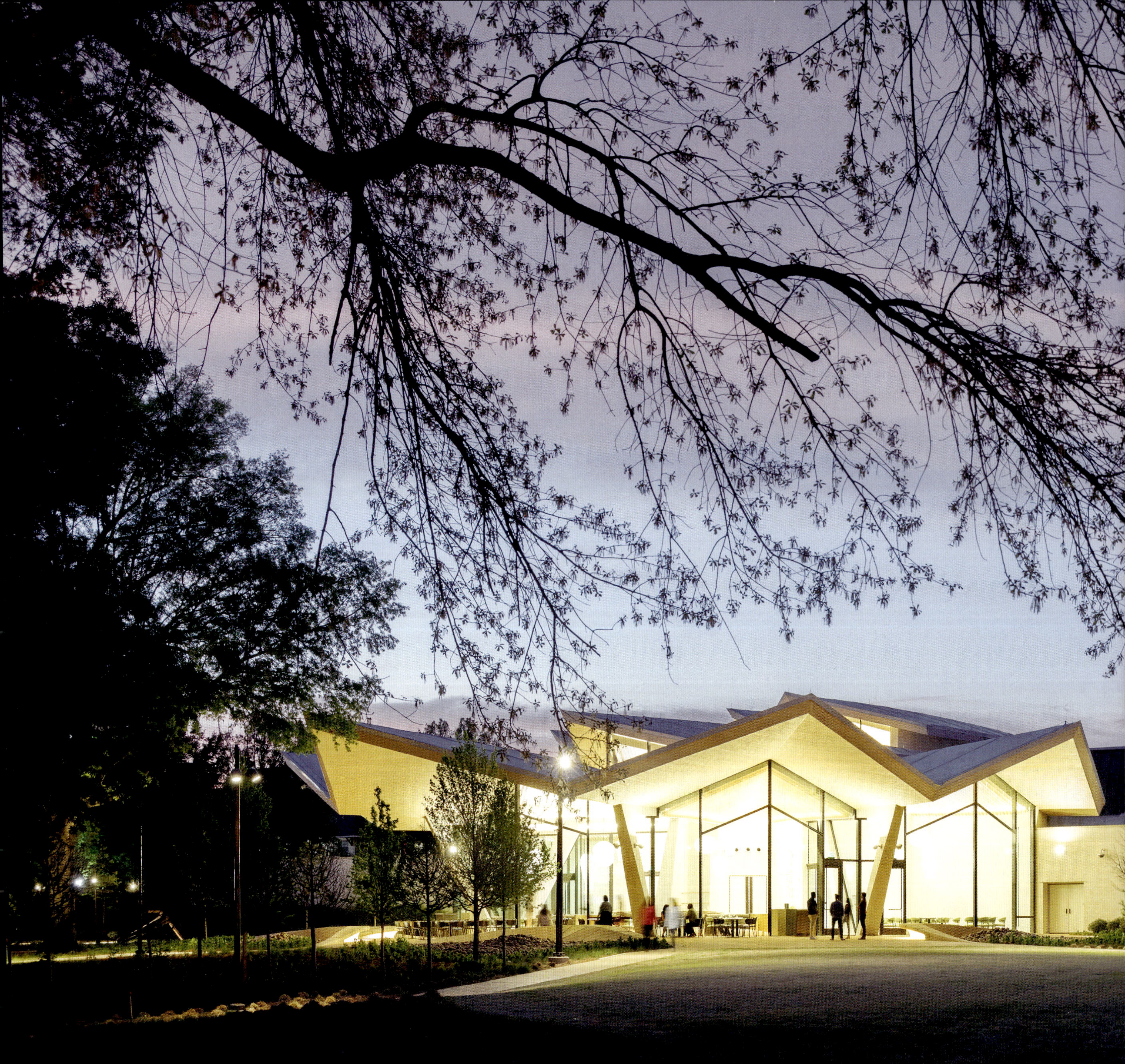

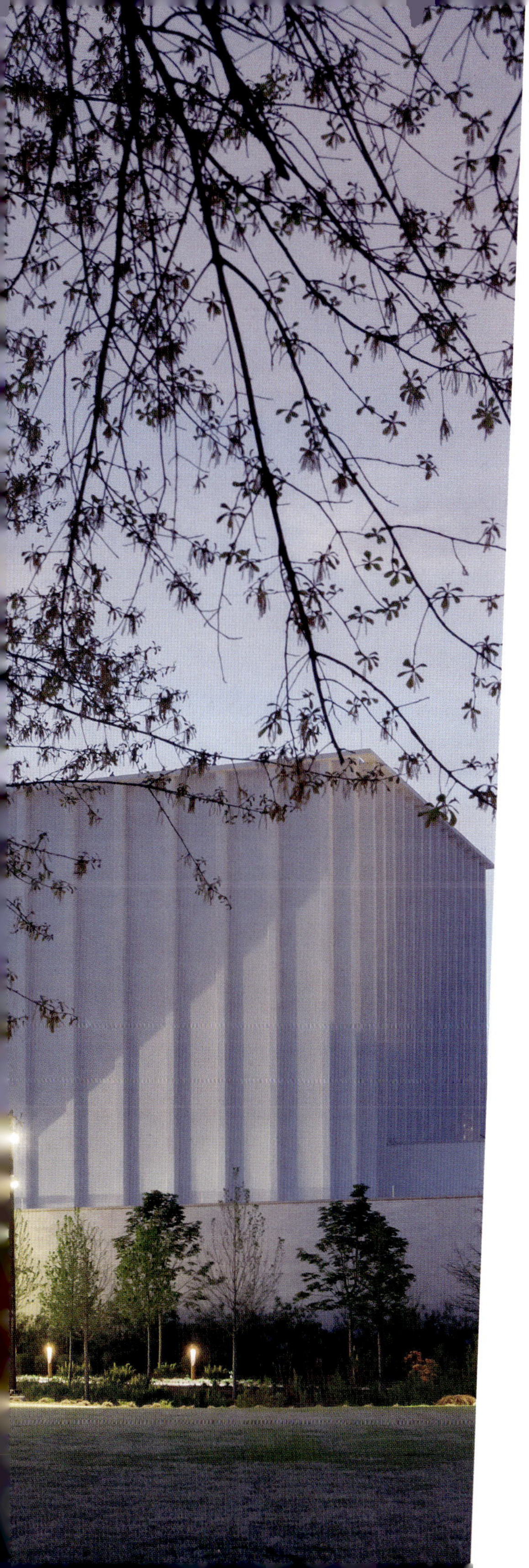

Looking to the Future

AMFA's mission is to create an inclusive cultural space that inspires and builds community through the visual and performing arts. By opening up to the surrounding neighborhood through floor-to-ceiling windows and extending the Museum's reach into MacArthur Park through outdoor social spaces, thoughtfully placed sculpture, and beautiful native plantings, AMFA welcomes its community in a novel way. The future promises memorable experiences for first-time visitors and renewed relationships with longtime supporters. This expanded audience is reflected in the Museum's diverse program offerings and collection acquisitions.

AMFA helps ensure a better future by caring for the natural world. The site's landscape includes more than 200 new native trees, such as oaks and wax myrtles, which will help increase biodiversity by providing habitat for birds and pollinators.

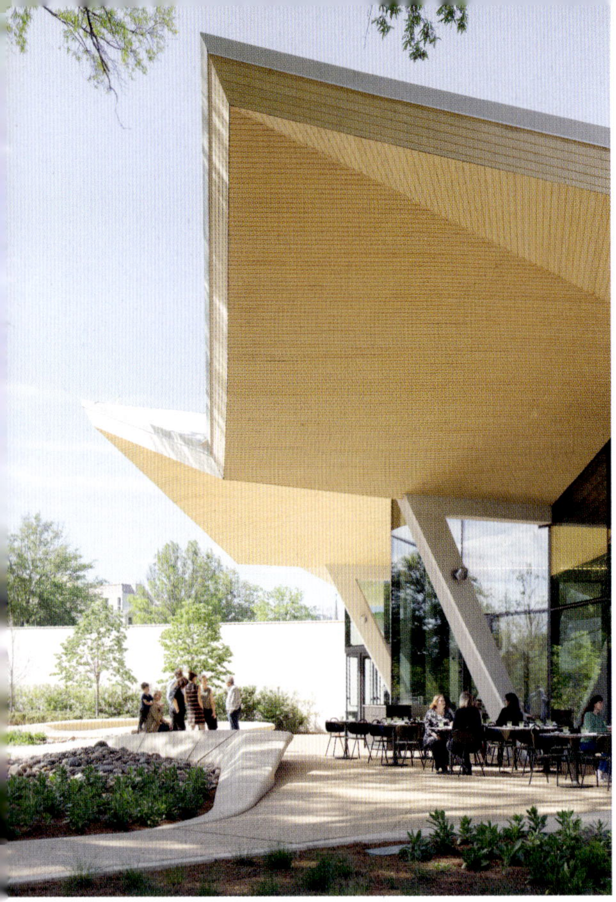

AMFA's open and welcoming architecture and grounds create harmonious indoor/outdoor spaces for socializing, relaxation, and contemplation.

The Museum building earned LEED Silver certification by reducing indoor and outdoor water use, optimizing energy performance, sourcing local materials, and enhancing indoor environmental quality. A "green building" rating system, LEED encourages new construction to reduce contributions to climate change and promotes the use of sustainable materials, among other goals.

Art museums steward permanent collections, ensuring that the works they protect last in perpetuity. This long-term responsibility does not exempt these institutions from adapting to serve different or changing audiences. AMFA's new design supports evolution for the unseen possibilities of the future. As society and technology shift, the building's flexible spaces will allow the Museum to respond accordingly. As artists invent new methods of creative expression, the galleries, Theater, Art School, and areas encouraging social interaction will accommodate tomorrow's methods of making, displaying, and experiencing art.

In reimagining a museum for the 21st century, SCAPE, Studio Gang, and AMFA created a building and surrounding landscape that will serve the residents of Little Rock and the state of Arkansas for decades to come. The future remains unknown, but one thing is certain—people will continue to connect with visual and performing arts—and one another—inside the thoughtfully designed AMFA.

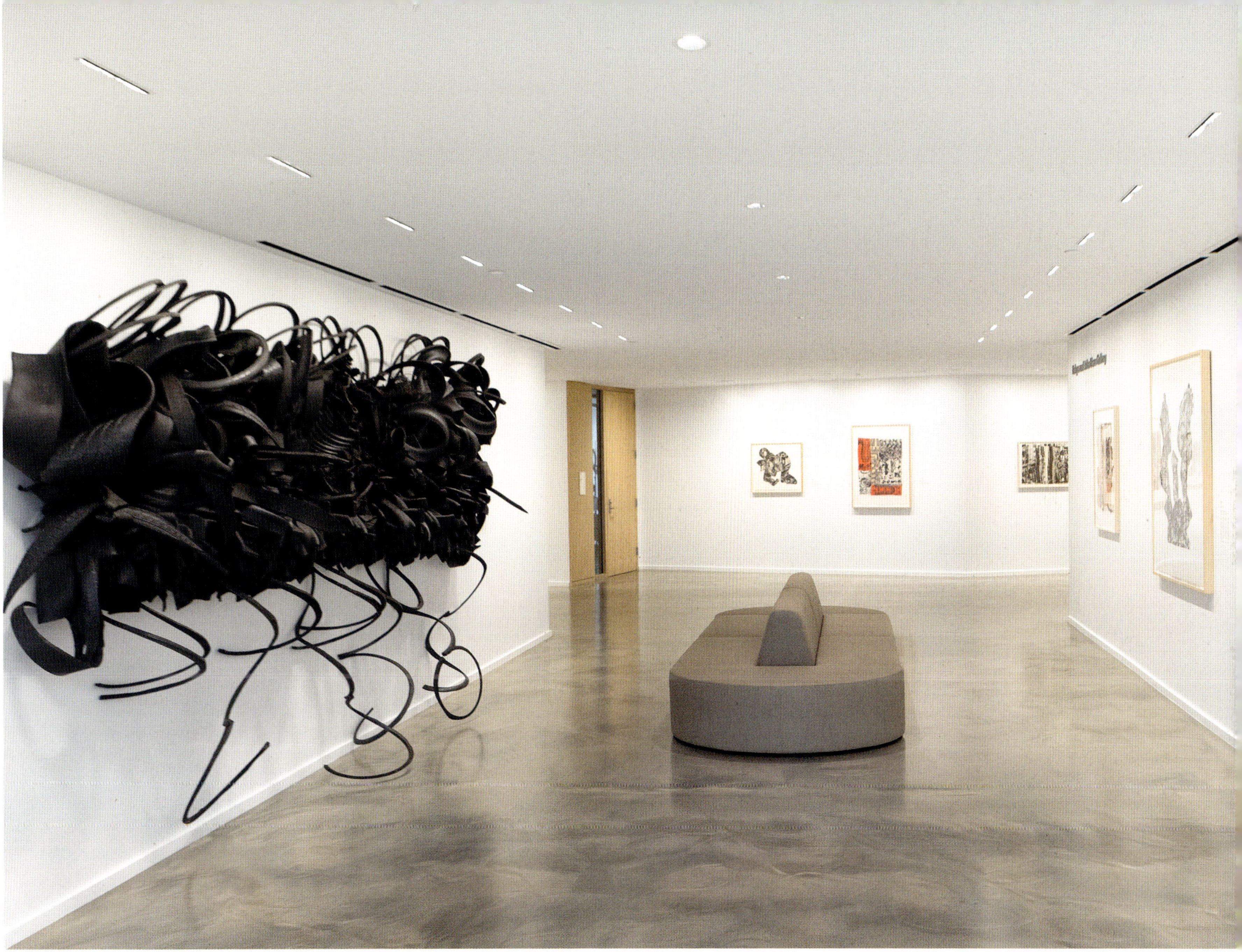

Chakaia Booker is best known for her large-scale sculptures made of sliced, twisted, and woven recycled tires. The inaugural exhibition of the Windgate Art School's Robyn and John Horn Gallery, *Chakaia Booker: Intentional Risks*, presented a 2007 sculpture by the artist, *The Fatality of Hope*, alongside lithographs and woodcuts she made in collaboration with master printers at the Robert Blackburn Printmaking Workshop.

SCAPE

Kate Orff, *Founding Principal and Partner*

Gena Wirth, *Design Principal and Partner*

John Donnelly, *Technical Principal and Partner*

Chris Barnes, *Studio Director, New Orleans*

Tanner Perrin, *Associate*

Polk Stanley Wilcox

David Porter, *Principal and CEO*

Cindy Pruitt, *Principal*

Acknowledgments

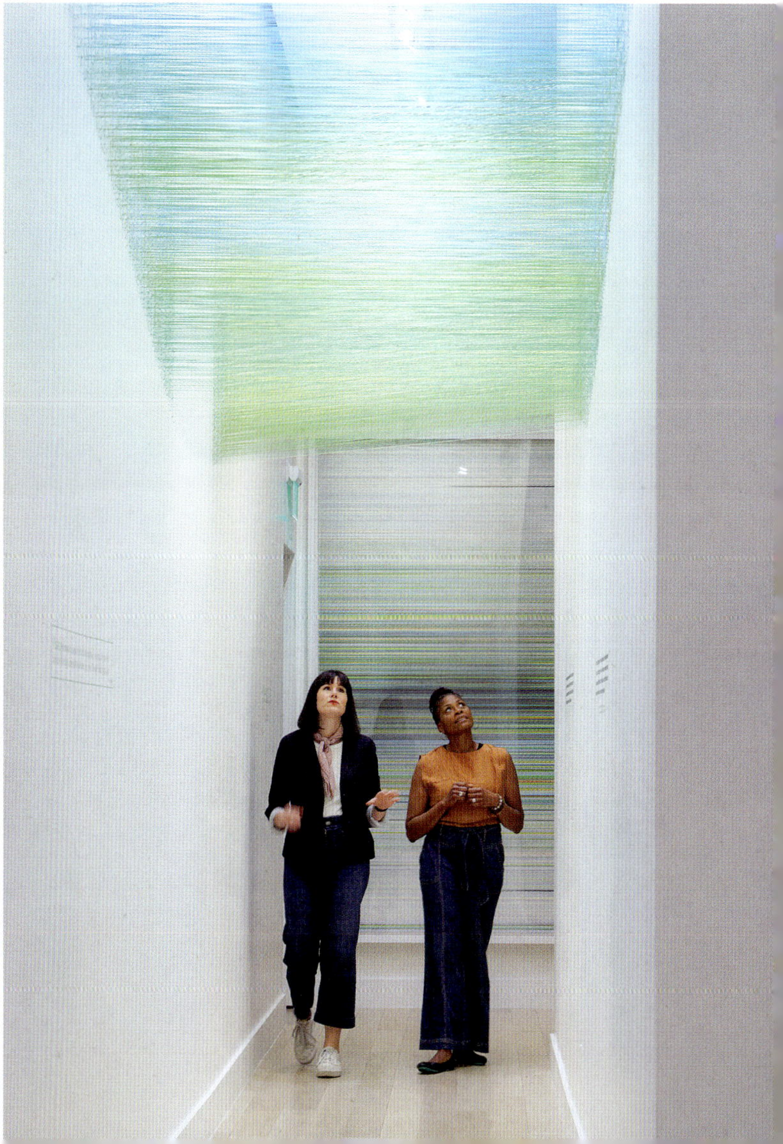

Anne Lindberg's *passage* (2023), a site-specific installation made with cotton thread, forms a luminous cloud of color in the Corridor. A hybrid passageway / gallery, the Corridor connects the Harriet and Warren Stephens Family Gallery to the Berta and John Baird Gallery.

Arkansas Museum of Fine Arts
in association with
Scala Arts Publishers, Inc.

First published in 2024 by
Scala Arts Publishers, Inc.
1301 Avenue of the Americas
10th floor
New York, NY 10019
scalapublishers.com
Scala – New York – London

Arkansas Museum of Fine Arts
501 East Ninth Street
Little Rock, AR 72202
arkmfa.org

Distributed outside Arkansas Museum
of Fine Arts in the book trade by
ACC Art Books
6 West 18th Street
4th Floor
New York, NY 10011

ISBN 978-1-78551-442-5

Editor:
Susan Higman Larsen

Design:
Diane Gottardi Graphic Design
Pennington, New Jersey

Printed and bound in China

Library of Congress Cataloging-in-Publication Data: a catalog record for this book is available from the publisher. Names: Ramirez, Victoria | Gang, Jeanne | Orff, Kate | Works. Selections. Title: Arkansas Museum of Fine Arts: Reimagining a Museum for the 21st Century / authors, Ramirez, Dr. Victoria D., Gang, Jeanne, Orff, Kate. Description: To mark the opening of refurbished Arkansas Museum of Fine Arts, in association with Scala Arts Publishers, Inc., 2024. Identifiers: LCCN 2023946511 | ISBN 978-1-78551-442-5 | Subjects: Arkansas | Architecture | Museums

PHOTOGRAPHY CREDITS

Image: Iwan Baan
Front cover, 2 – 3, 6, 10, 11, 12, 13, 15, 16, 17, 18, 19, 21, 22, 23, 24, 25, 26, 27, 28, 29, 30, 31, 32, 33, 58 – 59, 60, 63, inside back cover

Image courtesy of Jason Masters
4 – 5, 7, 34 – 35, 42 – 43, 61

Photography by Tim Hursley
8 – 9, 14, 20, 36

Photography by Ty Cole
40, 41

ARTWORK CAPTIONS

pp. 6, 11, 21
Henry Moore (Castleford, Yorkshire, England, 1898 – 1986, Perry Green, Hertfordshire, England), *Large Standing Figure: Knife Edge* (installation view), 1961, cast 1976, cast bronze, 140 ⅞ in., On loan from the City of Little Rock.

p. 13
Robyn Horn (Fort Smith, Arkansas, 1951 –), *Continuous Motion* (installation view), 2021, redwood with steel base, 73 x 59 x 15 in., Arkansas Museum of Fine Arts Foundation Collection: Given in honor of Robyn and John Horn for their generosity and commitment to the Arkansas Museum of Fine Arts with gratitude, Harriet and Warren Stephens, 2023. 2022.014.ab.

p. 18
Natasha Bowdoin (West Kennebunk, Maine, 1981 –), *Spring Song* (installation view), 2022 – 2023, acrylic on wood, gatorboard, and drywall supported with molded plastic brackets and aluminum pipe, 186 x 241 x 708 in., Commissioned by the Arkansas Museum of Fine Arts, 2022 – 2023. © Natasha Bowdoin.

p. 19
David Nash (Esher, Surrey, England, 1945 –), *Two Columns* (installation view), 2004, carved and burned redwood, shorter column: 192 x 60 in., taller column: 240 x 60 in., Arkansas Museum of Fine Arts Foundation Collection: Gift of Robyn and John Horn. 2021.010.002.1-2.

pp. 26, 27
Jesús Moroles (Corpus Christi, Texas, 1950 – 2015, Jarrell, Texas), *Broken Earth* (installation view), 2003, carved black granite on Texas pink granite base, 104 x 12 x 11 in., Arkansas Museum of Fine Arts Foundation Collection: Gift of Robyn and John Horn. 2021.010.001.

p. 31
Bernar Venet (Château-Arnoux-Saint-Auban, France, 1941 –), *Indeterminate Line* (installation view), 1994, rolled steel, 84 x 150 x 110 in., Arkansas Museum of Fine Arts Foundation Collection: Gift of Robyn and John Horn. 2021.010.003.

p. 61
Chakaia Booker (Newark, New Jersey, 1953 –), *The Fatality of Hope* (installation view), 2007, rubber (tires) and steel frame, 85 x 201 x 32 in., On loan from the artist, courtesy of David Nolan Gallery.

p. 63
Anne Lindberg (Iowa City, Iowa, 1962 –), *passage* (installation view), 2023, cotton thread and staples, 49 ½ x 312 x 53 ¼ in., Commissioned by the Arkansas Museum of Fine Arts, 2023.

Anne Lindberg (Iowa City, Iowa, 1962 –), *grene* (installation view), 2022, graphite and colored pencil on mat board, pressure adhered to diBond with a wooden framework edge, 108 ¼ x 63 ⁹⁄₁₆ x 3 in., Arkansas Museum of Fine Arts Foundation Collection: Purchase. 2022.011.